R-2967-RC

Foreign Area Studies in the USSR

Training and Employment of Specialists

Rose E. Gottemoeller, Paul F. Langer

January 1983

SANTA MONICA, CA. 90406

D1378068

PREFACE

In 1979, The Rand Corporation published a study of the supply of
and demand for foreign area specialists in the United States, focusing
on the uses to which their skills are put in the private and public
sectors.[*] The study, conducted at the request of the President's Commission on Foreign Language and International Studies, concluded that
in many sectors of the U.S. market the supply of specialists exceeded
the demand.

Rand then decided to fund a second study to examine the supply of
and demand for foreign area specialists in the USSR. This publication
reports the results of that study. The report presents a systematic
overview of the ways in which the Soviets respond to their own needs
for expertise in the international field.

In examining the Soviet case, Rand sought to answer several trou-
bling questions that emerged from the earlier work, including: To what
extent is the United States making the necessary effort to understand
the problems of foreign nations? To what degree should the average
U.S. citizen be educated in international issues? How can foreign area
specialists be used effectively in the United States? The Soviets have
answered similar questions for themselves, sometimes in ways that may
contribute to U.S. efforts to train and utilize foreign area specialists.

This study will be useful to policymakers concerned with the status
of international studies in the United States today, especially in regard to foreign language training and specialist utilization in unusual
country areas.

------

[*]Sue E. Berryman, Paul F. Langer, John Pincus, and Richard H.
Solomon, *Foreign Language and International Studies Specialists: The
Marketplace and National Policy*, The Rand Corporation, R-2501-NEH,
September 1979.

v

SUMMARY

This report presents a broad, systematic overview of the Soviet training and utilization of foreign area specialists. It examines in depth the specialists, their training, and their careers: in short, the human resources that contribute to Soviet military and economic power.

A much wider variety of careers is available to Soviet than to U.S. foreign area specialists. A 1979 Rand study noted a considerable lag in the United States between the number of people training for work in foreign affairs and those able to find jobs in the field.* We thought it important, therefore, to highlight in this study the many sectors of Soviet society that employ foreign area experts. The Soviet case provides some intriguing examples of how such expertise can fulfill many demands, particularly in areas where specialists could be better utilized in the United States.

We decided to look beyond the usual places where foreign area specialists find work--academia, for example--and explore the wide range of jobs in which Soviets deal with either foreign citizens or foreign information. Indeed, many of the people whom we describe are actually *double area specialists*: that is, they work in a field other than international affairs, but regularly use language and area skills.

The four sections of the report cover foreign language and area requirements in the Soviet general education curriculum; specialized foreign area training, primary through graduate school; utilization of specialists in ten sectors of the Soviet economy; and our conclusions about Soviet training and use of specialists, questions deserving further study, and Soviet innovations in the field that may apply to the United States.

Our data sources include European, U.S., and Soviet publications, Soviet emigre accounts, and interviews with U.S. specialists on the

---

*Sue E. Berryman, Paul F. Langer, John Pincus, Richard H. Solomon, *Foreign Language and International Studies Specialists: The Marketplace and National Policy*, The Rand Corporation, R-2501-NEH, September 1979, p. vii.

USSR. Unfortunately, a shortage of time, funding, and data prevented our going as deeply into the subject as we wished at many points during the research. We hope that readers will view our results as only a first step toward an understanding of the Soviet international field. If the interest warrants, this study could easily serve as the point of departure for a more systematic effort.

GENERAL FOREIGN AREA TRAINING OF SOVIET YOUTH

The Soviet education system assigns great importance to foreign area instruction, especially foreign languages. The language and area study curriculum for general education schools actually goes well beyond what is usually required at primary, secondary, and even college levels in the United States.

Ten years of education are standard and compulsory in the USSR system. Graduates of the tenth grade are said to have a complete secondary education and are eligible to apply for higher education at a university or institute, or for specialized technical training.

In the standard curriculum for primary-secondary schools, foreign language training begins in the fifth grade and continues through the tenth grade. The quality of instruction may vary, particularly in rural and ethnically non-Russian areas. In non-Russian-speaking areas of the USSR, Russian is taught as a foreign language in many schools. Officially, however, every Soviet schoolchild is required to study at least one foreign language, no matter what his career expectations.

Instruction in history and geography, the other foreign area subjects taught in Soviet schools, also follows a uniform curriculum throughout the USSR. Indeed, the prescribed subject texts can be found in any school in the country, translated into one of the 53 languages spoken by Soviet ethnic groups. Unlike many social studies curricula in the United States, Soviet history and geography courses emphasize foreign countries, albeit with a strong ideological bias. This bias is frankly acknowledged by political authorities as essential to a good Marxist-Leninist education.

Foreign languages continue to play a role in college-level education in the USSR, regardless of specialization. For example, physics students are required to take 300 hours of a foreign language, with no dispensation for computer programming or statistics as is often the case in the United States.

Other foreign area training at the university level is subsumed under the "social sciences." The Soviets include in this category politically oriented required courses such as Marxist-Leninist Philosophy and the Fundamentals of Scientific Communism. Thus, the ideological bias of general Soviet foreign area training continues during a student's higher education.

The most important conclusion that we can draw about the general foreign area training of Soviet youth relates not to ideology but to resources. By national plan, Soviet educators are creating year to year a huge pool from which to choose and nurture talent in the international field. Such talent is found in both those seeking careers as foreign area specialists and those who want to be physicists, mathematicians, and engineers. Thus, the USSR as a whole benefits from a valuable human resource that provides it access to the best that other countries have to offer--in any language and any field.

THE TRAINING OF SOVIET AREA SPECIALISTS

Specialized training for Soviet foreign and double area specialists can begin as early as primary school and continue through postgraduate studies. It can also include programs attached to professional schools, such as those sponsored by the Communist Party of the Soviet Union (CPSU) and the Committee of State Security (KGB).

Special language schools for grades one through ten offer the only differentiated academic curriculum for primary school students in the Soviet educational system. The schools supply linguistically proficient young people capable of being trained for jobs in various branches of the economy. Thus, the special schools are the earliest source of members for the USSR's pool of language and area specialists.

In 1976-1977, about 1 in 150 Soviet pupils attended special language schools, many of which are located in Moscow and Leningrad. Other areas of the country, particularly rural districts, apparently have few such facilities. The schools most frequently offer English, although the range of possibilities includes German, French, Hindu/ Urdu, and Chinese.

Not all graduates of the special language schools become diplomats or journalists. Many go into the publishing business as editors and translators. Others become librarians. Still others become scientists and engineers who are better able to follow western scientific developments because of their fluency in foreign languages.

Those who go on to higher education can continue to opt for specialized foreign area training at institutes and universities, or they can enter training programs for other fields while continuing certain types of language and area studies. The first group graduates as full-time foreign area specialists; the second group becomes double area specialists.

We describe several schools training foreign area specialists, but concentrate on the Moscow State Institute of International Relations (MGIMO), one of the top-ranking Soviet higher educational institutions. For the double area specialists, we concentrate on Moscow State University (MGU), the most prestigious university in the USSR.

Diversity is a significant factor in the training of Soviet foreign area specialists, but its value may be limited by the lack of direct exposure to the country of specialization. Soviet students do not routinely have opportunities to study and travel abroad.

Probably for this reason, the Soviets have developed a special practical training program. This internship program sends students from elite institutions, such as MGIMO, to countries as varied as the United States and North Yemen. There they work in embassies and other Soviet missions as probationers, or as translators or teachers in higher educational institutions. Thus, the Soviets apparently have found a means of exposing young and trustworthy foreign area specialists to life abroad. This practical training makes up--at least for a select few--for the isolation of international studies in the USSR.

We found that few courses in the agronomy and geology programs at Moscow State University are oriented specifically to conditions in foreign countries. The foreign language training that geology and agronomy students receive is probably their greatest asset in terms of foreign area expertise. Aspiring agronomists are required to study English for three years, and geologists study any of several foreign languages, also for three years. These strict language requirements probably are intended to help students to follow their specialty in foreign journals. However, they may also be intended to help geology and agronomy graduates work abroad and perform effectively as Soviet foreign aid technicians.

Outside formal training, many informal ways exist for drawing scientists, engineers, and others into the Soviet foreign affairs field. In recent years, for example, the social science institutes of the USSR Academy of Sciences have recruited engineering school graduates as apprentices in international studies. The resulting double area specialists are interested in topics such as western methods of applying computers to management. We suspect, however, that when the Soviet economy needs specialists who know about foreign technologies or methods, such specialists are trained, formally or informally, specifically for that purpose.

The professional schools of the Ministry of Defense, Ministry of Foreign Affairs, communist party, GRU (military intelligence), and KGB train senior double area specialists. These schools do not always award degrees, but they offer opportunities for their students to gain extra qualifications to advance their careers.

CAREER AND ROLE OF THE SOVIET AREA SPECIALIST

This section surveys the tasks and roles of Soviet workers trained in foreign language and area studies and employed in ten major areas of specialist activity: education, research, the media, government agencies, party organizations, the military, intelligence services, missions abroad, commercial enterprises, and international exchange organizations.

Where information was available, we describe each topic according to its international missions, the agencies that exist to fulfill those missions, and the role of the foreign area specialists employed in each. We also try to give readers an impression of what the individual jobs are like and what makes some of them more appealing than others to area specialists in the USSR.

Unfortunately, in many cases we were unable to look beyond the jobs to the qualifications and effectiveness of those who fill them. Furthermore, because the Soviets do not publish detailed employment figures on the field, we do not know the numerical distribution of specialists among academic, government, party, intelligence, and military organizations.

Given these limitations, we think that several trends are worth noting:

o   More Soviets, both civilian and military, are serving abroad today than in the past, and they are gaining exposure for the USSR, especially in the Third World.

o   A high level of educational attainment and professional polish is expected of those in the field, particularly in academia and the diplomatic service.

o   As Soviet foreign contacts have increased, the bureaucratic structures in ministries and other agencies have expanded to handle them.

Each of these trends has increased the Soviet demand for foreign area expertise.

Education

The Soviet statistical yearbook lists 174,000 language teachers, 100,000 geography teachers, and 166,000 history teachers working in day schools in the USSR during the 1978-1979 academic year. These figures do not include those working in night schools, those teaching more than one subject, and those teaching in higher educational institutions. Thus, it is obvious that there are many jobs in Soviet education for area specialists.

Language teaching jobs reportedly have declined in popularity. Young people tend to put language teaching in the same prosaic category as shop attendant and bank clerk. They try to avoid teaching assignments in rural areas.

Research Organizations

Over half of the social science institutes of the Soviet Academy of Sciences conduct research on the world outside the USSR. These institutes fall into two categories: area-specific institutes engaged in research on a particular country or world region and functional institutes dealing with key economic or political problems across national boundaries. Best known in the first category is the Institute of the USA and Canada (IUSAC); the second category is represented by the equally well-known Institute of World Economy and International Relations (IMEMO).

The international missions of the Academy of Sciences institutes mainly involve the production of information and analyses, although leading institute staff members are also responsible for presenting the Soviet perspective to the outside world. Three major trends have become apparent in the Academy's foreign area research over the past decade. First, Soviet foreign area research has refocused from linguistics and ethnography to the modern world and its problems. Government and party requirements have apparently forced this change.

Second, the growing Soviet political, economic, and military role in areas formerly outside the zone of Soviet interest has generated increased demand for specialists on previously neglected countries and regions. Finally, because the Soviets are committed to overtaking the western industrialized nations, Soviet specialists in the foreign area institutes are now systematically studying western organizational, administrative, and methodological concepts.

Outside the USSR Academy of Sciences, other Soviet organizations that conduct foreign area research include institutes attached to government ministries, universities, and academies of sciences in the Soviet republics.

The Media

Soviet international media activities include foreign news coverage, worldwide information-gathering, publication of literature on foreign nations, translation of foreign technical and scientific literature, and radio broadcasts in many languages and dialects. To perform these tasks, the Soviet media draw on a vast, diversified corps of specialists who combine professional training with linguistic and country expertise.

The two principal Soviet news agencies, TASS and Novosti, in addition to collecting and distributing news, make the preliminary evaluation of the information that they gather for political and propaganda purposes. Their large foreign affairs staffs thus must possess not only international expertise but also a high degree of sensitivity to shifting Soviet policy requirements.

Translation work also provides steady employment for thousands of foreign language specialists. Books, periodicals, and pamphlets intended for distribution abroad are published in some 50 languages.

Furthermore, in 1979 alone, almost 2000 foreign titles were translated into Russian and the many other languages used in the USSR. These translations were from some 100 foreign languages, although English dominated the group with about one-third of the titles translated--clearly a reflection of the special importance of English as the Soviets' channel to the outside world.

The international radio broadcasting service of the USSR is another major employer of foreign area expertise. The service broadcasts over 2000 hours a week in 63 languages, including 11 African languages. Afghanistan is currently a special target, receiving broadcasts in Dari as well as Pashto. There is also a 24-hour English service.

Government Agencies

Almost every ministry, state committee, and other national-level agency in the USSR shows some kind of international office in its administrative breakdown. Of necessity, our report examines only a limited number of offices in this large network employing foreign area specialists.

The USSR Ministry of Foreign Affairs carries out the traditional tasks of diplomacy, including important legal, consular, and policy-planning functions. It also has at least one functional office not usually found in western foreign ministries. This office, the Administration for Servicing the Diplomatic Corps, provides basic services--for

example, maids and chauffeurs, theater tickets, and driver's licenses--
to foreign diplomats in Moscow. The administration's personnel have
some knowledge of foreign languages--at least enough to eavesdrop--and
also are trained in intelligence functions. Thus, the Ministry of
Foreign Affairs needs both foreign area specialists and double area
specialists.

The State Committee for Science and Technology, whose official
mission is not international, also employs many full-time foreign area
specialists. Some of these employees have degrees from prestigious
educational institutions and most have excellent knowledge of at least
one foreign language. The committee requires such skills to administer
the many scientific cooperation agreements that the USSR maintains with
countries around the world.

The most important function of the State Committee for Science and
Technology, however, is to manage the USSR's acquisition of foreign
technology. Therefore, it employs many double area specialists trained
in foreign languages and the sciences who investigate foreign technologies and judge which have importance for the USSR.

Party Organizations

The Politburo of the CPSU Central Committee is the paramount collegial organ for the formulation of Soviet foreign policy. The research to back up Politburo decisions is performed in the Central Committee apparatus, which is therefore an important employer of foreign
area specialists.

The Central Committee departments that contribute to the making of
Soviet foreign policy include Cadres Abroad, International, International Information, and Liaison with Communist and Workers' Parties of
Socialist Countries. Our discussion of the role that foreign area specialists play in party organizations concentrates on the activities of
the International Department.

The International Department works behind the scenes in the Soviet
decisionmaking process, gathering information and making a case for a
particular policy direction. Because department personnel brief the Politburo directly, they exercise a very important influence on Soviet

foreign policy. The department employs about 150 well-educated, highly qualified foreign area specialists in Moscow.

Military Organizations

Soviet military activities in the foreign affairs field involve both research and military service abroad. Our discussion of research concentrates on the General Staff Academy, one of several military institutes that conduct foreign area research. Our discussion of military foreign service concentrates on the various services Soviet military personnel perform abroad.

The General Staff Academy, the foremost military research institute involved in foreign area studies, receives its research tasks directly from the Minister of Defense and the Chief of the General Staff. Researchers at the academy must possess two types of foreign area expertise: language training and basic understanding of western military science. Strategic arms limitation is one particular area in which the academy has apparently contributed a considerable body of research.

In 1979, almost 16,000 Soviets and Eastern Europeans were serving abroad as military advisers in the Third World. The Soviets were engaged in training local personnel, working directly with them on weapon use and maintenance. We do not know whether these Soviet military aid technicians receive any language or area training before they are sent to a developing country. Nor do we know how well they mix with their Third World clients. In short, we do not know much about their effectiveness as representatives of the Soviet system.

Intelligence Services

The Committee for State Security and Soviet military intelligence pervade all dealings between the USSR and foreign countries. They must therefore employ more foreign and double area specialists than any other organization in the USSR. To the full-time intelligence officers must be added thousands of specialists attached to other agencies who may be called on to work for the intelligence services.

KGB and GRU officers are highly skilled professionals and members of an elite cadre. If trained to work abroad, they know the languages, culture, and society of their specialty country. The intelligence services, like other Soviet agencies employing foreign area specialists, put a premium on skills in unusual foreign languages.

Many KGB and GRU jobs for which foreign area skills are needed resemble similar jobs in western intelligence services. However, the Soviets' approach to research and analysis differs somewhat from that of their western counterparts. The Soviets appear to place more emphasis on collecting raw intelligence than on evaluating it. Hence, skilled intelligence officers are probably considered more useful in the field, collecting information, than at home, evaluating it.

Because the KGB and GRU offer such perquisites as elite status and travel abroad, they attract some of the best talent produced by the Soviet educational system. As specialists with language and area skills, young intelligence officers can expect to make excellent careers in the international field. For them as for many of their peers in other agencies, language and area skills are the key to interesting work, promotion, and success.

Missions Abroad

Each Soviet embassy is responsible, at least in a formal sense, for an interlocking network of missions involved in aid programs, trade, propaganda, diplomacy, and intelligence. Many missions in Soviet embassies around the world apparently have an intelligence function at least as important as their stated purpose. In addition, the KGB and GRU staff virtually all embassies and missions to international organizations.

Since the late 1960s, the International Department of the CPSU Central Committee has also assigned personnel to important Soviet embassies abroad. International Department representatives collect information about political parties, assess the political situation in the country concerned, and establish contacts with local organizations and individuals. They reportedly occupy positions of great importance in the embassies where they are located.

Soviet foreign affairs specialists also serve abroad in international institutions. The largest number serve in the United Nations, including in UNESCO, the International Labor Organization, the Economic Commissions for Europe and the Far East, and the International Atomic Energy Agency. The USSR also enjoys the benefits of three delegations --the Soviet, Ukrainian, and Belorussian--to the United Nations.

Commercial Enterprises

The USSR's economic interaction with the non-Communist world has grown steadily in scope and volume in recent years. Official Soviet statistics put total Soviet trading partners at close to 100. The large and diversified administrative apparatus that supports those activities provides a major source of international specialist employment.

The Soviet Ministry of Foreign Trade operates a large bureaucracy staffed with experts, including a substantial number of specialists on international economics and foreign market analysis, many with expertise on particular countries. Permanent trade missions in the major trading nations serve as its instrument abroad. At the same time, short-term survey or negotiating teams often travel to the West to negotiate large-scale deals that cannot be handled by the permanent missions.

The USSR has long been operating a number of sales and representational offices abroad, including the Narodnyy Bank, Intourist, TASS, and Aeroflot. All employ Soviet foreign language and area specialists.

Aeroflot routinely keeps its own ticketing agents and maintenance crews in the countries that it serves, rather than hiring local personnel as many large international carriers do. We do not know precisely how much language and area training these employees receive before they are sent abroad. Ticketing personnel, at least, can speak as many as four languages.

Outside the USSR, the Soviets have shown increased interest since the mid-1970s in acquiring equity in foreign countries. This trend has brought an outward flow of managerial talent from parent organizations in the USSR, since the Soviets seem to prefer maintaining operational control of companies that they wholly or partly own. A high-level manager can expect to spend at least one extended tour abroad and may in the course of a career work in several foreign countries. As a result, he becomes an experienced international businessman.

Inside the USSR, the Soviet government does not allow foreign firms to acquire control of Soviet enterprises. It permits instead various types of cooperative ventures, all of which were designed to keep Soviets in control. Projects typically involve a long-term relationship with foreign partners, perhaps involving updates in plant technology over time. Thus, Soviet plant managers have to employ staff capable of serving as liaison with their western counterparts for an extended period.

International Exchanges

Around the world, the USSR has entered into agreements for cooperation in areas as different as fisheries, industrial development, science, education, and culture. Thus, Soviet foreign area specialists fill many positions in exchange administration. Because we have the most information about Soviet cooperation agreements with the United States, we focus on that exchange relationship.

Academia is the best-established area of Soviet-American exchange cooperation. Scholars began traveling between the two countries in 1956-1957, and the procedure became formalized with the signing of the Soviet-American Exchange Agreement in 1958. Science and technology exchange agreements, administered on the Soviet side by the State Committee for Science and Technology, are also well established. Other forms of exchange cooperation include university-to-university exchanges, language study programs, foreign policy seminars, and citizen group exchanges.

All Soviet organizations involved in exchanges require language-skilled personnel, facilities, and procedures to handle foreign visitors. When we include other countries of the world in the network of exchanges, the size of this bureaucratic structure becomes apparent. Functions that private organizations perform in many countries are all within the purview of the Soviet government.

CONCLUSIONS

The research described in this study has led to four major conclusions about the training and utilization of foreign area specialists in the USSR. After presenting these conclusions, we indicate questions that remain unanswered and suggest a few areas where the Soviet experience may be applicable to the United States.

First, we found that the Soviet foreign language and area training effort is enormous, officially extending to every schoolchild. Thus, Soviet educators have a huge pool of talent from which to choose candidates for specialized foreign area training. Such training is an extremely well-developed system that produces fluent linguists and knowledgeable specialists, often in exotic areas of the developing world.

Second, the foreign area specialty is one of the few Soviet professions that legitimizes contacts with foreigners and travel abroad. Thus, the profession offers perquisites that attract high-caliber young members of Soviet society. Their career choice, further, is made relatively risk-free by the secure demand for foreign area specialists in the USSR.

Third, the Soviet system recognizes the need for numerous Africa, Latin America, China, and Middle East specialists on a regular basis. Thus, the secure demand for specialists in a large number of areas, some of which are exotic, ensures a trend toward diversity in the Soviet international field.

Finally, the large group of double area specialists in the USSR reflects Soviet efforts both to counterbalance a closed society and to benefit from other countries' successes. The Soviets go to great lengths to ensure their supply of double area specialists. An aspiring Soviet scientist is required to study foreign languages systematically, usually for three years.

Assimilating western technology is only one purpose for these efforts. The Soviets also use double area specialists to study western business practices and military theories, among other things. Specialist activity in many sectors of the Soviet economy suggests that detailed knowledge of western processes exists in the USSR across a spectrum of special areas.

Several questions emerged during our research that we were unable to answer within the scope of this study. A recurring question concerns the overall issue of effectiveness. We know that the Soviets send military and aid technicians abroad, for example, but we do not know how effective they are at forging friendships for the USSR around the world.

Full answers to the question of the effectiveness of Soviet aid personnel are not easy to come by. However, we feel that it would be possible to develop useful partial answers through those who have come into contact with Soviets, particularly in developing countries. U.S. diplomatic and aid personnel, businessmen and bankers, technicians employed by commercial firms, and recent Soviet emigres are all potential sources of information.

Our second question concerns the distribution of double area specialists among the sectors of the Soviet economy. We suspect that sectors employing large numbers of double area specialists--for example, management theory, computers, and chemicals--are sectors of particular Soviet interest. We would like to know what other sectors employ them and why. Businessmen and embassy commercial officers who have worked with Soviets might be able to provide such information. Another source is the literature of the various fields. Abundant coverage of western literature in Soviet technical journals would provide evidence of double area specialist activity.

Our final question returns to the matter of effectiveness and concerns an important limitation in the Soviet training and utilization of foreign area specialists. Only a few elite aspiring foreign affairs specialists are sent abroad for practical experience during training. Once graduated, these same people are again apparently the only members of the field likely to travel outside the USSR. Most Soviet foreign area professionals, in other words, never visit the countries in which they specialize. Because of this limitation, we wonder how effective such specialists can be in interpreting the outside world to Soviet society.

Of course, we can never completely resolve this issue, especially since we are looking at the Soviet international field through western eyes. Soviet policymakers evidently are satisfied with their foreign area specialists: they continue to utilize them in large numbers. From the Soviet point of view, their window on the world is at least adequate and perhaps excellent.

What benefit can the international field in the United States derive from the Soviet experience of training and utilizing foreign area specialists? Clearly, some Soviet uses of the profession would be unnecessary or inappropriate in the U.S. context. It would probably be a waste, for example, to replicate the legions of Soviet double area specialists who follow foreign scientific developments. Because the communication network among scientists in the West is fairly well developed, in most cases U.S. scientists need not be double area specialists.

The adoption of certain Soviet practices, however, might help U.S. scientists, policymakers, and others. For example, we think that the double area specialist phenomenon gives the Soviet government flexibility that would be useful in the U.S. context as well. Soviet policymakers can turn for information directly to Soviet double area specialists in a number of fields, rather than depending on internationalists who may not have specialized knowledge.

Furthermore, more language-skilled graduates in the sciences would provide U.S. policymakers with the raw material for developing double area expertise in the scientist population when the demand for such expertise arises. In other words, we think that developing potential capability in this sphere may be as important as developing actual capability.

Aspects of Soviet foreign area training are also useful for U.S. policymakers to consider. For example, we described how certain foreign area institutes sponsor internships in Soviet embassies and missions abroad. The apparent scale of these internship programs would be difficult to duplicate in the U.S. case, because the structure of the foreign service and the expense of housing in foreign capitals dictate against it. Likewise, embassy-connected internships would not be necessary in many places where students can easily travel--Western Europe, Latin America, Japan. The internships would be most useful in countries that limit student travel--the USSR, China, some countries of Africa.

A student serving as an intern in Moscow probably could not do the type of academic research that exchange scholars do, because he would not have access to libraries and archives. However, he would be gaining practical experience by living and working in the city and by performing free services for the Department of State or other sponsoring agency.

An informal internship arrangement has existed in Moscow for years. Many foreign diplomatic families there hire young women from their home country to work as nannies for one or two years. These young women use their free time to perfect their Russian, explore Moscow, and learn about Soviet life. Often, they later enter the Soviet field professionally. Expanding and adapting such a program on an official or semiofficial basis would be complicated, but we think not impossible.

Obviously, training and utilization of foreign area specialists is a diverse, well-developed system in the USSR. It may not always work precisely, but it does produce a varied array of specialists on a regular basis, and then uses them. This lesson, we feel, is the basic one of our research, and the most important.

ACKNOWLEDGMENTS

We thank the many people both in and out of government who have
helped us to research this study. Our special thanks are due to Harry
Gelman of The Rand Corporation, Seymour Rosen of the Department of
Education, Steven Grant of the International Communications Agency,
Allen Kassof and Daniel Matuszewski of the International Research and
Exchanges Board, Blair Ruble of the Woodrow Wilson International
Center for Scholars, John Dziak of the Defense Intelligence Agency,
and Robert Legvold of the Council on Foreign Relations. The notes to
the text contain the names of many others without whose help this task
would not have been possible. Needless to say, we are entirely responsible for the views expressed.

CONTENTS

GLOSSARY

CMEA	Council of Mutual Economic Assistance
CPSU	Communist Party of the Soviet Union
FBIS	Foreign Broadcast Information Service (U.S.)
GKES	State Committee for Economic Relations with Foreign Countries (USSR)
GKNT	State Committee for Science and Technology (USSR)
GRU	Main Intelligence Administration (USSR)
IA	Institute of Africa (USSR)
IDV	Institute of the Far East (USSR)
ILA	Institute of Latin America (USSR)
IMEMO	Institute of World Economy and International Relations (USSR)
IUSAC	Institute of the USA and Canada (USSR)
IVAN	Institute of Oriental Studies (USSR)
KGB	Committee of State Security (USSR)
Komsomol	Communist youth organization (USSR)
MFA	Ministry of Foreign Affairs (USSR)
MFT	Ministry of Foreign Trade (USSR)
MGIMO	Moscow State Institute of International Relations (USSR)
MGU	Moscow State University (USSR)
MPA	Main Political Administration of the Soviet Army and Navy
NIKI	Scientific Research Marketing Institute (Ministry of Foreign Trade USSR)
RSFSR	Russian Soviet Federated Socialist Republic

SALT	Strategic arms limitation talks
SRF	Strategic Rocket Forces (USSR)
TASS	Telegraph Agency of the Soviet Union
UNESCO	United Nations Educational, Scientific, and Cultural Organization
UpDK	Administration for Servicing the Diplomatic Corps (Ministry of Foreign Affairs USSR)

INTRODUCTION

Soviet military, economic, and intelligence assets are usually examined in terms of hardware, infrastructure, and financial or natural resources. This report explores for the first time in depth the human aspect of the USSR's international capabilities. It provides a wide-ranging, systematic examination of the ways in which the Soviets meet their needs for expertise in the international field.

The scope of the study imparts a detailed impression of the many types of foreign area expertise available to Soviet leaders. When considering personnel for a project abroad, a Soviet decisionmaker can choose from among specialists trained in foreign affairs and from among specialists whose foreign area expertise complements another profession.

The study looks beyond the usual places where foreign area specialists find work--academia and diplomatic service--to explore jobs in which Soviets deal either with foreign citizens or foreign information. Specialists in a field other than international relations who regularly use language and area skills are referred to here as "double area specialists." These specialists either travel abroad or remain at home to manage commercial relations, information processing, cultural exchanges, and many other types of interaction.

Section I of the study describes general foreign area training in the USSR. An examination of the foreign language, history, and social science requirements of the educational curriculum in use country-wide provides an idea of what the Soviet population as a whole is being taught. Section II explores specialized foreign area training at all levels of the Soviet educational system, for both full-time foreign area specialists and double area specialists. Section III discusses the career and role of the Soviet area specialist in ten major sectors in which international specialists find work in the Soviet system. Section IV reflects on the significance of foreign area training and employment in the USSR, identifies trends in the Soviet use of foreign area specialists, and notes important differences in U.S. and Soviet attitudes toward the field. In this final section, we also suggest ways to answer several questions that recurred throughout the study. Finally, we describe innovative methods that the Soviets have used to solve problems in the field, methods that could be adapted for use in the United States.

Our study draws on Soviet reports, statistics, and journal articles; Soviet emigre accounts; U.S. and European sources; and interviews with U.S. specialists on the USSR. Unfortunately, time and funding constraints, as well as the incomplete nature of Soviet data, prevented our going as deeply into the subject as we wished at many points during the research. We hope that our results will be viewed as a first step toward comprehensive understanding of the Soviet international field. This study could serve as the point of departure for a longer range, more systematic effort if interest on the part of potential users should warrant it. We are confident that more could be done with regard to data collection and analysis.

I. GENERAL FOREIGN AREA TRAINING OF SOVIET YOUTH

In the past two decades, the USSR has emerged from the international isolation of the Stalin era to play an increasingly active role in world affairs. However, the nature of the Soviet regime requires that it severely control its citizens' contact with foreign nations, nationals, and ideas so as to ensure internal stability. These conflicting considerations obviously create a policy dilemma for the training of specialists in international affairs, an activity essential to the operations of any major advanced nation. The handling of the conflict with regard to Soviet international specialists is discussed throughout this report.

The conflict between foreign area training and the control of foreign contacts arises also, if to a lesser extent, in Soviet general educational policy. Should Soviet youth be acquainted with conditions in foreign nations and should they be taught foreign languages, even when they are not destined to enter specialized careers where such knowledge is essential?

One might assume that the Soviets would want to limit their young people's exposure to knowledge about foreign areas. Yet our findings suggest otherwise: the Soviet school assigns importance to foreign area instruction and especially to the teaching of foreign languages, English above all. Soviet foreign language instruction apparently extends well beyond that usually encountered in American elementary or high schools, and even beyond the college curriculum for those not embarking on a specialist career.

Seymour M. Rosen, an outstanding U.S. authority on Soviet education, characterized the teaching of languages and related subjects as follows:

> The Soviets clearly give their pupils a distorted, ideological, stereotyped view of world reality rather than objective data. What should not be underestimated, however, while maintaining awareness of their serious flaws, is the breadth of Soviet programs in world understanding—Communist style—and in foreign languages. These programs

reach the broad spectrum of Soviet public school pupils and
students in higher education. They serve as vehicles of
mass indoctrination, while at the same time preparing youth
for their role as citizens in the Soviet state and as representatives of that society in the world community.[1]*

Available school and university curricula prescribed by the relevant USSR education ministries illustrate the present state of foreign
language and area training in Soviet schools and institutions of higher
learning. In line with Soviet policies in all areas of social and economic activity, standards and requirements generally apply nationwide
(with some modifications for non-Russian ethnic populations, primarily
with regard to the language of instruction, but not touching on subject
content). The system provides little flexibility for course options
and for a sampling of various unrelated subject matters. The curricula
tabulated below reflect the actual course requirements that Soviet students must fulfill to earn the certification and diploma necessary for
obtaining work.

The standard curriculum for elementary and secondary schools in-
troduces foreign language instruction in the fifth grade and continues
it throughout the ten-year course of study now standard and compulsory
in Soviet education (see Table 1). In principle, a pupil may choose
one of several languages. In practice, however, many or perhaps most
Soviet schools teach only one foreign language, usually English (the
most commonly taught), German, or French. After the tenth grade, further language training depends on career choice.

Once students complete the tenth grade, they may enter a university or institute, or a secondary specialized school for technical or
vocational training. The policy of requiring foreign language study of
many students in secondary specialized schools who will not go on to a
university or other higher academic education is surprising. The required curriculum for a physician's assistant (*fel'dsher*) clearly shows
foreign language instruction to be an important part of the required

---

*Notes to the text appear at the end of each chapter.

Table 1

STANDARD CURRICULUM IN PRIMARY AND SECONDARY SCHOOLS

Subject	Periods per Week per Grade									
	1	2	3	4	5	6	7	8	9	10
Russian Language	12	11	10	6	6	4	3	2	–	1
Literature	–	–	–	2	2	2	2	3	4	3
Mathematics	6	6	6	6	6	6	6	5	6	6
History	–	–	–	2	2	2	2	3	4	3
Social Studies	–	–	–	–	–	–	–	–	–	2
Nature Study	–	1	2	2	–	–	–	–	–	–
Geography	–	–	–	–	2	3	2	2	2	–
Biology	–	–	–	–	2	2	2	2	1	2
Physics	–	–	–	–	–	2	2	3	4	5
Astronomy	–	–	–	–	–	–	–	–	–	1
Technical Drawing	–	–	–	–	–	–	1	2	–	–
Chemistry	–	–	–	–	–	–	2	2	3	3
Foreign Language	–	–	–	–	4	3	3	2	2	2
Art	1	1	1	1	1	1	–	–	–	–
Music and Singing	1	1	1	1	1	1	1	–	–	–
Physical Education	2	2	2	2	2	2	2	2	2	2
Labour Training	2	2	2	2	2	2	2	2	2	2
Elementary Military Training	–	–	–	–	–	–	–	–	2	2
Total periods per week for compulsory subjects	24	24	24	24	30	30	30	30	32	34
Options	–	–	–	–	–	–	2	3	4	4

NOTE: A new course, Principles of the Soviet State and Law, was in-
troduced into the form 8 timetable in September 1975.

SOURCE: *Sbornik prikazov i instruktsii Ministerstva prosveshcheniya
RSFSR, 1972*, no. 11, 2. Adapted from John Dunstan, *Paths to Excellence
and the Soviet School*, NFER Publishing Co., Windsor (Berkshire), UK,
1978, p. 39.

training (see Table 2). This requirement is apparently absent from
certain vocational school curricula, for example, that for electri-
cians. Of course, such students have already received foreign language
instruction during the preceding elementary and secondary phase of
training, as have *fel'dsher* trainees.

The success of Soviet language instruction cannot be determined
without a more extensive search of Soviet literature than we have been

Table 2

SECONDARY SPECIALIZED SCHOOL CURRICULUM:
3½-YEAR *FEL'DSHER* COURSE

Cycle and Subject	Total Hours	In Class	Laboratory and Practical Work
General education cycle			
Chemistry	156	110	46
Foreign Language	170	170	
History	170	170	
Literature	188	188	
Mathematics	300	300	
Physics	194	166	28
Principles of Scientific Atheism	16	16	
Social Studies	68	68	
General medical cycle			
Anatomy	154	112	42
Biology	78	60	18
Health Care Organization	36	20	16
Hygiene	68	50	18
Latin	76	76	
Microbiology	80	58	22
Pathological Anatomy and Pathological Physiology	95	70	25
Pharmacy and Prescription Writing	163	121	42
Physiology	100	74	26
Special cycle			
Diseases of Ears, Nose, and Throat	64	26	38
Diseases of Teeth and Oral Cavity	48	24	24
Epidemiology	90	40	50
Eye Diseases	64	26	38
Infectious Diseases	154	84	70
International Medicine and Patient Care	390	170	220
Nervous and Emotional Disturbances	72	32	40
Obstetrics and Gynecology	290	120	170

SOURCE: Seymour M. Rosen, *Education in the USSR--Research and Innovation*. Office of Education, Washington, D.C., 1978, p. 27.

able to conduct and without interviews with a broad cross-section of individuals who have gone through the Soviet educational process. We know from numerous Soviet reports, however, that the quality of instruction in this as in other school subjects is uneven.

Rural schools tend to be seriously disadvantaged, as are the schools in many ethnically non-Russian areas. In ethnic schools, the language of instruction may be Russian, but it is more likely to be the local language, with Russian required as a second language. In addition, students are officially required to study a non-Soviet foreign language.

Unofficially, however, language requirements seem to be quite lax in many ethnic regions, even in regard to Russian. For example, Central Asians, Kazakhs, and Azerbaydzhanis apparently are often inducted into the army at the age of 18 with little or no knowledge of Russian—especially if they are from rural areas.[2] We must, therefore, be somewhat skeptical about the quality of foreign language instruction for many non-Russian ethnic groups in the USSR, despite official curriculum requirements.

What influences a student's perspective on the outside world perhaps more than languages is the general foreign area training he receives during his school years. At the elementary and secondary (ten-year compulsory) level, no subject is devoted exclusively to international affairs. The Soviet school system, like that in other countries, takes up such topics within the context of broader study categories, primarily history, geography, literature, and social studies (see the subject listings in Tables 1 and 2, above).

We did not study the detailed course requirements for each of these subjects, nor do we know to what extent they are available. We know, however, that instruction in a subject must follow an extremely detailed outline specified by the relevant ministry and that compliance with these outlines is monitored. We assume, therefore, that foreign content of the four subjects listed above is substantial.

Two aspects of foreign area instruction in Soviet schools are especially striking. First, Soviet teaching places heavier emphasis on geography and history, and within these subjects on the foreign content, than American teaching. Second, while some degree of ideological bias is to be expected in any educational system, in the Soviet case such bias is frankly acknowledged by the highest political authority and encouraged as an essential element of good Marxist-Leninist education.

Prescribed history and geography texts, which are uniform for the entire USSR and appear in as many as 53 of the languages spoken there, contain obvious bias. A recent comparative study of U.S. and Soviet textbooks concludes that Soviet texts focus on the least attractive aspects of American life and treat all western nations as similarly "imperialist." However, the study also concludes that the texts are carefully researched and that the facts (rather than concepts) and statistical data in them are remarkably free of error.[3]

We cannot estimate the effect of Soviet foreign area instruction on the outlook of the typical Soviet graduate. We believe, however, that he is likely to emerge from the education system with some knowledge of the outside world and in that sense is perhaps better equipped than his American counterpart.

Foreign language and area training in Soviet higher education receives the same degree of attention that it gets in secondary and lower-level professional training—in distinct contrast to conditions in the United States. Foreign language instruction continues to play a role in most specializations.

The Soviet planning system closely links educational training at all levels to the economic and technological requirements of the Soviet state. At the higher levels, each professional curriculum is assigned a specialty code number that appears in the overall Soviet economic plan, and personnel requirements are established for that specialty. Qualified students are admitted to higher education and trained for a specific career according to quotas fixed in the national economic plan.

Once admitted to undergraduate or early postgraduate training in a Soviet university or other institution of higher education—called a *vyssheye uchebnoye zavedeniye*, or *vuz*—the student must follow a prescribed curriculum. Tables 3 to 5 show the curricula for Russian Language and Literature, History, and Physics, respectively.

Table 3

CURRICULUM FOR SPECIALTY 2001: RUSSIAN LANGUAGE AND LITERATURE

Qualifies Students for Career of Philologist and Teacher
of Russian Literature; Term of Study: Five Years

Subject	Total Hours	Lectures	Labo- ratory Work	Seminars, Practical Studies
History of Philosophy	40	40	--	--
Logic	40	30	--	10
Foreign Language (occidental or oriental)	500	--	--	500
Latin	110	--	--	110
Psychology	50	40	10	--
Pedagogics	70	70	--	--
Methods of Teaching Russian	60	30	--	30
Methods of Teaching Literature	60	30	--	30
Introduction to Linguistics	70	40	--	30
General Linguistics	50	40	--	10
The Old Slavic Language	70	30	--	40
Russian Dialects	50	30	--	20
History of the Russian Language	190	120	--	70
Modern Russian	450	140	--	310
Practical Stylistics (the Russian language)	70	10	--	60
Introduction to Literary Studies	70	40	--	30
Theory of Literature & Principles of Marxist-Leninist Aesthetics	70	60	--	10
Russian Folklore	50	40	--	10
History of Russian Literature	430	330	--	100
History of Foreign Literature	320	300	--	20
Soviet Literature	130	130	--	--
Subjects Related to Particular Republics (Russian, native languages, literature, history, etc.)	280	100	--	180
Specialization Subjects	490	160	--	330
Physical Training	140	--	--	140
History of Soviet Society	170	70	--	100
Marxist-Leninist Philosophy	130	50	--	80
Political Economy	110	40	--	70
Principles of Scientific Communism	70	30	--	40
Total	4340	2000	10	2330

SOURCE: Seymour M. Rosen, *Education in the USSR--Current Status of Higher Education*. Office of Education, Washington, D.C., 1980, p. 21.

Table 4

CURRICULUM FOR SPECIALTY 2008: HISTORY

Qualifies Students for Career of Historian and Teacher
of History and Social Sciences; Term of Study: Five Years

Subject	Total Hours	Lectures	Laboratory Work	Seminars, Practical Studies
History of Philosophy	50	50	--	--
Logic	40	30	--	10
Psychology	50	40	10	--
Pedagogics	70	70	--	--
Methods of Teaching History & Social Sciences	60	40	--	20
Latin	100	--	--	100
Foreign Language	500	--	--	500
Fundamentals of Archaeology	70	60	--	10
History of Primitive Society	40	40	--	--
Fundamentals of Ethnography	70	50	--	20
Ancient History	170	120	--	50
History of Middle Ages	170	120	--	50
History of the USSR	520	340	--	180
Modern & Recent History	400	260	--	140
History of Asian and African Countries	280	200	--	80
History of the Southern and Western Slavs	100	100	--	--
Source Authorities of the History of the USSR	50	50	--	--
Historiography of USSR History	50	50	--	--
Auxiliary Historical Subjects (paleography, historical geography, numismatics, etc.)	100	50	--	50
Subjects Related to Particular Republics (history, ancient language, native language and literature, etc.)	230	110	--	120
Specialization Subjects	470	270	--	200
Physical Training	140	--	--	140
History of Soviet Society	200	100	--	100
Marxist-Leninist Philosophy	140	80	--	60
Political Economy	140	70	--	70
Principles of Scientific Communism	70	30	--	40
Total	4280	2330	10	1940

SOURCE: Seymour M. Rosen, *Education in the USSR--Current Status of Higher Education*. Office of Education, Washington, D.C., 1980, p. 22.

11

Table 5

CURRICULUM FOR SPECIALTY 2016: PHYSICS

Qualifies Students for Career of Physicist
Term of Study: Five Years

Subject	Total Hours	Lectures	Labo- ratory Work	Seminars, Practical Studies
Foreign Language	300	--	--	300
Chemistry (special course)	70	30	40	--
Elements of Technical Drawing	70	12	58	--
Elements of Radio- electronics	106	34	72	--
Higher Mathematics				
Mathematical Analysis	510	240	--	270
Analytical Geometry & Higher Algebra	120	70	--	50
Methods of Mathematical Physics	140	100	--	40
Computers & Program- ming	80	40	20	20
General Physics				
Mechanics, Molecular Physics, Electricity, Optics	380	240	--	140
Atomic Physics	110	70	--	40
Nuclear Physics	70	70	--	--
Practical Work in Physics	530	--	530	--
Theoretical Physics				
Theoretical Mechanics	120	70	--	50
Electrodynamics	120	80	--	40
Quantum Mechanics	120	100	--	20
Thermodynamics & Sta- tistical Physics	120	90	--	30
Specialization Subjects	530	410	--	120
Specialization Laboratories	550	--	550	--
Physical Training	140	--	--	140
History of Soviet Society	170	70	--	100
Marxist-Leninist Philosophy	130	50	--	80
Political Economy	110	40	--	70
Fundamentals of Scientific Communism	70	30	--	40
Total	4666	1846	1270	1550

SOURCE: Seymour M. Rosen, *Education in the USSR--Current Status of Higher Education.* Office of Education, Washington, D.C., 1980, p. 23.

As shown in Table 5, the Soviet educational system places strong emphasis on continued language training even for physicists. Language-skilled Soviet scientists are not unusual--most of the better ones are reported to know several languages. Likewise, foreign area training, in addition to languages, at the university level is included under required subjects like Marxist-Leninist Philosophy, Political Economy, and Fundamentals of Scientific Communism.

The foreign language and area training program for the Soviet population, even if imperfectly implemented in certain areas of the country, thus provides Soviet planners with a huge pool from which to choose and nurture talent in the international field. Good language students can be encouraged to pursue careers as in the international field, and science students with language aptitudes can be encouraged to perfect their skills so as to follow western developments in their fields. As a result, Soviet leaders have certain talents and capabilities available to help them make decisions regarding the world outside the USSR.

Section I Notes

1. Seymour M. Rosen, *Soviet Programs in International Education*, U.S. Department of Health, Education, and Welfare, Washington, D.C., 1975, pp. 2-3. See also Dr. Rosen's *Education in the USSR--An Annotated Bibliography of English-Language Materials, 1965-1973*, Office of Education, Washington, D.C., 1974. Useful data are also found in John L. Scherer (ed.), *USSR--Facts and Figures Annual*, Academic International Press, Gulf Breeze, Florida, published annually since the mid-1970s and in the substantial periodical literature on the subject. An extensive literature published in the USSR in Russian deals with virtually every conceivable aspect of Soviet education. Some useful statistical data are contained in the annual *Narodnoye khozyaystvo* and in other more specialized handbooks.

2. S. Enders Wimbush and Alex Alexiev, *The Ethnic Factor in the Soviet Armed Forces*, The Rand Corporation, R-2787-NA, March 1982, pp. 74-75. See also Martha Brill Olcott, "Soviet Muslims and the Military," in Gregory Varhall and Kenneth Currie (eds.), *The Soviet Union: What Lies Ahead?* Government Printing Office, Washington, D.C., forthcoming.

3. See "Mid-Term Report of the US/USSR Textbook Study Project," Howard D. Mehlinger, Project Director, Indiana University, Bloomington, January 1980 (unpublished).

II. THE TRAINING OF SOVIET AREA SPECIALISTS

INTRODUCTION

A typical Soviet foreign affairs specialist arriving in the United
States in 1979 on an exchange between the USSR Academy of Sciences and
the American Council of Learned Societies would have had excellent academic credentials. Almost certainly he would have attended school in
Moscow and received a graduate degree from a prestigious Soviet insti-
tution--the Moscow State Institute of International Relations (MGIMO),
Moscow State University (MGU), or an institute of the Academy of Sciences. He would have spoken English well and probably claimed knowledge
of another language--perhaps one as exotic as West African Bambara. Finally, his specialization would have stretched far beyond linguistics to
the study of sinology, U.S. oceans policy, criminal law, or any of doz-
ens of other major current subjects.[1]

This academic specialist, of course, represents but one category
of those employed in the foreign affairs field in the USSR. Other categories embrace those involved in military and economic aid, intelligence, journalism, diplomacy, trade, translation--the list goes on.

This section considers the specialized training that people in foreign-area-related jobs receive in the Soviet educational system in special primary schools, graduate and postgraduate training, and professional schools attached to entities like the Committee of State Security
(KGB) or communist party. For each type of institution, we review to
the extent possible student selection criteria, curricula, faculties,
locations, and facilities.

The section ends with an assessment of the programs and a comparison with related efforts in the United States. We also highlight at
that point gaps in our information and questions deserving further
study.

SPECIAL LANGUAGE SCHOOLS

Special language schools for grades one through ten have the only
differentiated curriculum for primary school students in the Soviet

educational system, except for the well-known music, ballet, and art schools.[2] The concept grew from a resurgence of interest in foreign languages during World War II. At that time, the USSR lacked enough foreign language speakers to staff its diplomatic service and trade missions abroad. The language schools thus were intended to supply such cadres in fairly short order. As John Dunstan put it, "The purpose of the special schools is . . . to supply linguistically proficient young people who will be trained for jobs in various branches of the economy."[3]

In 1976-1977, about 1 in 150 Soviet pupils, living mostly in Moscow and Leningrad, attended special language schools.[4] Other areas of the USSR, particularly rural districts, apparently have fewer specialized language schools. Thus, a young Leningrad resident's chances of entering a special language school in 1969 were seven times greater than those of his peers elsewhere in the Russian Republic (RSFSR).[5] While there, he was most likely to have studied English, although German and French were also good possibilities. If interested in the exotic, he may have entered the Hindi/Urdu or the Chinese school. Spanish and Italian were also available.[6] His parents, however, would probably have been anxious to enter him in an English program, because English would be most useful to the future career of their eight-year-old.

Special language schools have been described as prestigious institutions reserved for children of the Soviet elite. Dunstan believes that although the schools are prestigious, their "reserved" nature has been exaggerated. Precisely because of their differentiated curriculum, he states, parents feel that they offer children a chance for a better education in an otherwise totally uniform system. Hence, the schools have gained prestige because they are different and better not because they are attended by the elite.[7]

Selection Criteria

Dunstan suggests that the various language schools do not follow uniform admission procedures. The only routine requirements seem to be that the child be in good health and free of speech defects.[8] The procedure may involve special tests for which students prepare during nursery school and kindergarten--a process familiar in Japanese society

but seemingly out of place in the egalitarian Soviet system. In other
cases, schools apparently admit students with no formal tests. Such
schools may be new ones, or they may teach languages less desirable
than English.[9]

Soviet writers have more than once portrayed admission procedures
at the most sought after schools, and Dunstan gives several amusing examples. The best was written by a Soviet newspaper correspondent who
likened the testing day at a special language school to the annual admissions commotion at Moscow State University:

> Smartly turned-out children go before an incomprehensible
> and consequently still more terrifying committee, whose
> job it is to find out their aptitude for foreign languages
> by listening to their poems and hearing them describe lit-
> tle pictures. True, in a few years' time the shy little
> boy may prove to be a polyglot, and the forthcoming little
> girl to be not really so gifted after all. But at present
> she is the one enrolled in the school.[10]

The correspondent's last comment points to the dilemma that Soviet
educators face with the special school program. As long as there are
not enough such schools to admit every student who wants to attend, educators must use some kind of selection criteria. Dunstan feels that
the schools at least try to select on the basis of promise and not parental influence, or *blat*, as influence is called in the USSR.[11]

If the special language school network expands, it will have to do
so with no loss of quality; otherwise, the program will no longer fulfill its mission.

School Policy, Curriculum, and Faculty

Students in special language schools spend two to four hours a
day more in class and several hours a day more on homework than do their
counterparts in regular Soviet schools. The curriculum is intense and
competitive, and students who do not perform up to standards are weeded
out and sent to ordinary, less desirable schools.[12]

The extra hours of classroom work are devoted to foreign language
study. No more than 14 students are assigned to a class, whereas in

regular schools a class may contain more than 25. This more favorable student-teacher ratio provides the basis for effective language teaching emphasizing oral exercises as well as grammar. In regular schools, grammatical theory dominates language teaching, and children do not develop skill in speaking. The special language schools obtain much better speaking results. Dunstan states that he "as well as many other visitors can testify to the fluency and purity of accent which even pupils in the middle forms display."[13]

In addition to the extra hours of foreign language study, other subjects such as mathematics and physics may be taught in a foreign language.[14] This practice was to have been a major feature of special schools when they first were planned, but several limitations have prevented its widespread adoption.

The first limitation stems from the dearth of qualified teachers capable of teaching specialized math and science concepts in a foreign language. Although higher pedagogical institutes in the USSR offer method courses in these areas, apparently they have not been able to keep up with demand as the network of language schools has grown.[15]

The second limitation involves the lack of textbooks and other teaching aids needed for such courses. According to Dunstan, standard Soviet textbooks had often in the past simply been translated into foreign languages. The vocabulary of these books was often much too difficult for the level of language skill that the students had attained. Dunstan notes, however, that the situation is apparently changing, and more textbooks and teaching aids are being produced especially for the language schools.[16]

The final limitation involves the obstacle that a foreign language can become to the broad comprehension of mathematics, science, and other less abstract subjects such as history. If a student's knowledge of the foreign language is imperfect, he will probably not understand all the nuances of the concepts being presented to him. Imagine, for example, the difficulty that a sixth grade student would have grasping Newtonian physics taught in English in his first physics classes. No matter how skillful his teacher, the student would have studied English for only four years and his vocabulary would probably be too narrow for complete comprehension.[17]

In sum, special language schools occupy a unique place in the Soviet educational system. They are the only schools offering primary school students a chance to study foreign languages intensively for nine years. Because they are different, they are sometimes criticized for engendering elitism in parents and children. Dunstan, however, argues persuasively that parents prefer the schools simply because they improve the child's chances for the future. While his future is being ensured, the child develops into an excellent linguist, thus fulfilling the main purpose for which the schools were established.

Not all graduates of the special language schools become diplomats or journalists. Many go into the publishing business as editors and translators. Others become librarians. Still others become scientists and engineers who are better able to follow western scientific developments because of their fluency in foreign languages.

HIGHER EDUCATION

A special language school student may take one of several paths once he completes his first ten years of training. He may enter a higher educational institution (*vuz*; plural *vuzy*); he may go to a four-year technical high school (*tekhnikum*), where, because he has already completed ten grades, he will be admitted to the eleventh grade; or, he may go directly to work in a job that may or may not use his foreign language skills.

Dunstan reports that in 1968, graduates of four special English schools in Moscow and Leningrad made the following career choices: 26.5 percent entered *vuzy* training teachers, translators, and other foreign affairs specialists; 39.2 percent entered scientific and technological *vuzy*; 11.9 percent entered *tekhnikum*s; 8.1 percent went directly into English-related jobs, and 14.2 percent took jobs requiring no language skills.[18]

In this section, we consider the two types of students who go on to higher education in the Soviet system: those who enter the diplomatic

service, journalism, linguistics, and other traditional international
fields and those who specialize in disciplines like economics, physics,
or geology but who must receive foreign area training for a particular
job--the double area specialists.[19] These students are usually the
more competitive, gifted, and well placed, for not all who aspire to
higher education can be admitted.

For the traditional foreign area specialists, we concentrate on
the Moscow State Institute of International Relations, which has
launched many eminent foreign affairs experts. A measure of MGIMO's
importance can be seen in the number of its graduates who were nominated
to be sent to the United States on the Academy of Sciences/Council of
Learned Societies exchanges from 1978 to 1980. Of the 63 Soviet nominees, 20 had attended MGIMO. We also have a colorful picture of MGIMO
from graduates like Aleksandr Kaznacheev and Vladimir Sakharov, who have
since defected to the West. Because their accounts may not be entirely
free of bias, we will mesh their stories with information from other
sources. We will also describe some of the other institutions that
train Soviet internationalists.[20]

For the double area specialists, we concentrate on Moscow State
University, the most prestigious university in the USSR. Twenty of the
1978-1980 exchange nominees attended MGU at some time in their academic
careers, a figure that confirms Moscow's preeminence as an educational
center for the foreign affairs field. Because so many major subjects
could be considered part of a double area specialty, we chose two to
exemplify the concept: agronomy and geology.

The professional schools attached to the KGB, Communist Party of
the Soviet Union (CPSU), Ministry of Foreign Affairs, and armed forces
are discussed in the final portion of this section. Such professional
schools do not always grant a *vuz* diploma to graduates of their programs; nevertheless, they are often important stepping-stones in an individual's career.

We include under higher education work leading to the undergraduate
degree (*diplom*) and to the graduate degrees (*kandidat* and *doktor*).[21]
Students can go directly from a ten-year program in a special language

school to a higher educational institution such as MGU or MGIMO. An individual's chances for admission may be better, however, if he works for two years before applying to a *vuz*. The advantage of working is discussed further below.

MGIMO and the Internationalists

The experience of getting into MGIMO differed for Aleksandr Kaznacheev and Vladimir Sakharov. Kaznacheev went to the institute when it was first formed in the mid-1950s. He had good grades but no influential friends, and he suspects that he was admitted because of his unique interest in the Burmese language. Soviet leaders had just turned their attention to the Third World, and they needed well-trained cadres versed in exotic languages. Kaznacheev benefited from this sudden need, and his admission to MGIMO seemed almost automatic.[22]

Less than ten years later, Vladimir Sakharov required a master plan to gain entry into the same school. Luckily for him, his father was not only influential but also personally acquainted with the school's director of admissions. This man told Sakharov exactly how to prepare for the competition:

> Beyond having the right connections, I had to have a superior academic record, graduating with at least what in the U.S. would be an A-minus average in all required subjects --politics, history, geography, languages, literature, science. In addition, I had to have a good sports record and have taken part in competition. Naturally, I had to be a model Communist youth, with officially approved tastes, conduct, and interests. For the entrance interviews, I had to develop poise, and quickness of mind, and be ready with the right answers for any situation. Finally, I had to prove I was a real Communist worker. This could be accomplished either by volunteering to do work for the Komsomol (Communist Youth Organization) or by holding a job for two years.[23]

Sakharov followed this regime for almost four years. He got a part-time job as a lab technician in a secondary school and went to school at night. He took part in amateur rowing competitions and placed third in the Moscow championships--good enough, as he put it, to qualify for MGIMO.[24]

Toward the end of this period, the admissions director warned
Sakharov to cut back on playing jazz records, listening to the Voice of
America, and using taxis, for he would be under surveillance. Evidently he cleared all the hurdles, however, and he was called for a preexamination interview. This interview, along with the entrance exams,
proved to be *pro forma* in his case, although they apparently serve as
tools for weeding out less desirable candidates.[25]

Sakharov's high school experience reinforces the point made earlier, that a Soviet student need not attend a prestigious special language school to gain entry into a prestigious higher school. In fact,
Sakharov attended night school with 30- to 40-year-old blue collar
workers who were trying to complete their secondary education. For
admission to MGIMO, grades, political reliability, sports record, and
influence were more important than the school attended.

Blat seemed to be almost vital for MGIMO entry in Sakharov's day,
and Kaznacheev also indicates that it played an important role in his
time. The same has been said of other prestigious institutions that
train Soviet foreign affairs specialists, especially the institutes of
the Academy of Sciences. For example, Galina Orionova, another defector, reports that "our family is nowhere nearly important enough for me
to get into the really exclusive institutions."[26] Like Kaznacheev, she
managed to win a place at a newly formed institute, the Institute for
U.S. Affairs of the Academy of Sciences, now called the Institute of
the USA and Canada (IUSAC). Nowadays, she reports, she would have been
automatically excluded because positions are reserved "for the children
of very exalted families."[27]

According to Jan Triska and David Finley, *blat* has become a permanent fixture in the admissions process: "There is an official criterion
of 'social worthiness' to which character recommendations are obliged to
address themselves. Its ambiguity offers a place for 'social class' to
take effect."[28] However, *blat* does not seem to be an invariable factor
in the selection process.

Robert Legvold notes that *blat* notwithstanding, both IUSAC and the
Institute of World Economy and International Relations (IMEMO) of the
Academy of Sciences apparently recruit graduate students from

universities around the country. This process is particularly evident
when the institutes are trying to establish new in-house areas of
expertise.

Legvold has seen a five-year trend toward recruiting and training
in-house specialists on politico-military strategy at IUSAC. He feels
that catching an institute's attention is a critical step--one that can
be accomplished through imaginative research and native intelligence
rather than through parental influence.[29]

Other, unwritten selection criteria may operate at the prestigious
foreign affairs institutes. For example, Sakharov reports that, no
matter how intelligent and capable, a woman would never have gotten
into MGIMO without her father's influence. He also notes that Jews in
the student body were "allowed no mistakes," suggesting that Jews were
not welcome at the school.[30] The importance or extent of such criteria
is open to conjecture.

MGIMO is located in an imposing building on Krymskaya Square in
central Moscow. It originally housed a military school for the aris-
tocracy and still maintains aristocratic marble hallways, parquet floors,
and a pillared conference hall.[31] The student body that emerges from
the selection process is also imposing, formed as it is of young people
on their way up in the Soviet system.

We know little about MGIMO's current faculty. Both Kaznacheev and
Sakharov describe the high quality of the instruction they received,
and Sakharov recalls attending classes and lectures given by the foremost Soviet experts in fields like international law.[32] An idea of the
range of specialists represented on the faculty may be gained from
Table 6. The source of this table, the CIA *Directory of USSR Ministry
of Foreign Affairs Officials*, lists many more MGIMO faculty members,
but without specialty.

Blair Ruble has noted that although MGIMO is a teaching institute
and not a research center, many of its professors participate in major
research projects. These projects often come about, according to Ruble,
because of the strong informal ties that exist between MGIMO and IMEMO.[33]

As a teaching institute, MGIMO offers a number of undergraduate and
graduate degree programs,[34] with specializations in Chinese linguistics,

Table 6

MGIMO FACULTY MEMBERS LISTED BY SPECIALITY, 1980

A. A. Akhtamzyan	Reader; specialist in Soviet–German relations
I. P. Blishchenko	Professor, Chair of International Law
N. P. Bogdanova	Senior instructor; English
V. N. Danilenko	Senior instructor; English
G. V. Fokeyev	Docent; specialist on Africa
M. A. Khrustalev	Docent, Chair of International Relations and USSR Foreign Policy; specialist on contemporary history of the Arab countries
F. I. Kozhernikov	Professor; Head, Chair of International Law
N. A. Lapteva	Teacher; English
S. N. Lebedev	Professor; Head, Civil Law and Procedure Department; also employed by Ministry of Foreign Trade
A. V. Meliksetov	Professor; specialist on modern China
P. V. Milogradov	Professor; specialist on Near and Middle East and Africa
M. A. Mogunova	Docent; specialist on law
V. I. Moskovchenko	Professor; Chair of History of International Relations and USSR Foreign Policy
L. G. Pamukhina	Teacher; English
V. D. Shchetinin	Professor; Dean, Faculty of International Relations
E. V. Tadevosyan	Head, Chair of Scientific Communism
V. G. Trukhanovskiy	Professor; Head, Chair of International Relations and USSR Foreign Policy

SOURCE: National Foreign Assessment Center, *Directory of USSR Ministry of Foreign Affairs Officials*, Central Intelligence Agency, No. CR 80-13493, August 1980, pp. 31-33.

economics of colonial and dependent countries, economics of imperialist countries, history of international relations and foreign policy, history of modern times, Indian philosophy, international law, international trade and USSR foreign trade, and law of bourgeois states.[35]

In addition, Sakharov reports that a new faculty of international journalism was established at MGIMO in the mid-1960s. Its program emphasized propaganda through radio, television, and press and work among local political leaders, religious organizations, and correspondents. According to Sakharov, only the best-placed students were accepted into the program, which was directed by a Central Committee official.[36]

Both Kaznacheev and Sakharov indicate that a number of exotic languages are taught at MGIMO. Kaznacheev describes in some detail the language requirements in the mid-1950s:

> An intensive language training course was made a key part of the whole Institute program. The requirement is stiff —a thorough knowledge of at least two foreign languages —one the language of the country of specialization, and the other the foreign language most often used there. Two Western languages are taught in the Western division, and one Eastern and one Western language in the Eastern division. The students of the Eastern division specializing in India and Pakistan provide a good example. They are split into three groups and study Hindi and English, Urdu and English, and Bengali and English. As a rule, almost half of them pick up another Indian language, such as Tamil or Gujarati. The students in the Arab group study Arabic and either English or French, often both of them. The Afghan group study three languages: Pushtu, Persian, and English.[37]

Sakharov's experience ten years later confirmed that the system was continuing to operate as Kaznacheev described it. Sakharov was first assigned to the Southeast Asian section and studied Vietnamese and French. Later he switched to a Middle Eastern specialization and studied Arabic and English.[38]

The general teaching policy of MGIMO appears to differ in important ways from the policy in other Soviet *vuzy*. It apparently depends less on rote learning and theory and more on pragmatic issues and discussion. For example, Sakharov recounts that "The economic training was quite thorough and was focused upon the practical, day-to-day workings of financial operations rather than on theories."[39] Kaznacheev is even more specific: "Unlike other 'ordinary' Soviet colleges, where political studies are nothing but a thoughtless and formal droning of a few

officially prescribed and superficial textbooks, political subjects are
studied in [MGIMO] in great detail and by the method of analysis, discussion, and argument."[40]

A major revision of the institute's curriculum in the mid-1960s
placed greater emphasis on business and commercial subjects, according
to Sakharov. The earlier program had stressed diplomatic protocol,
international law, foreign criminal codes and local regulations, intelligence tactics, languages, and military strategy. After the change,
Sakharov depicts a curriculum that includes western banking and currency
systems, business procedures, corporate structure, principles of international trade, accounting, securities, marketing, and labor relations.[41]

In sum, MGIMO stands out among higher educational institutions in
the USSR. Its teaching methods and curriculum, including foreign language studies, are exotic by Soviet standards. Its faculty members are
known experts in their fields and in many cases are closely tied to important research institutes. Its graduates are virtually assured of interesting and prestigious work in Moscow or in a Soviet mission abroad.

Its prominence enables MGIMO to select students with superior academic and extracurricular records. It turns out sophisticated, well-
educated foreign affairs specialists for academia, the diplomatic service, intelligence organizations, and the media. Thus, it apparently
serves as the entry level of the old boy network in the Soviet foreign
affairs establishment. Because of the success of its graduates, it
attracts a student body with influential parents eager to guarantee
their children's future.

Lumumba University

Patrice Lumumba Peoples' Friendship University lies at the other
end of the Soviet higher education spectrum from MGIMO. Established in
1960, Lumumba University provides university training free of charge to
students from Africa, Asia, the Middle East, and Latin America.

When under the Khrushchev regime the interest of Soviet leaders
focused on the Third World, large numbers of Third World students were
admitted to Soviet higher education programs. Soviet universities and
institutes, however, could not always meet the needs of these students.

Rosen writes, for example, of "the difficulty such students experienced
in adjusting to regular Soviet university work in classes attended predominantly by Russian students and with course content shaped to the
[Soviet] background."[42] The rationale for Lumumba University emerged
from these needs.

Students arriving from the Third World spend one year in the university's preparatory faculty, where they receive intensive Russian language training and remedial work to bring their secondary educations up
to Soviet standards.[43] After that, the students enter one of six faculties: engineering, agriculture, medicine, physics-mathematics and natural sciences, history and philology, or economics and law.[44]

The programs last from five to seven years, the longest being medicine.[45] They are geared to foreign students, with small classes and a
great deal of individual instruction. The curricula, in fact, are
matched to individual students and the needs of their home countries.
The emphasis rests on practical applications of the knowledge acquired.
For example, whereas regular Soviet engineering curricula may emphasize
architecture, the Lumumba curriculum emphasizes hydraulic machinery and
water supply and drainage techniques.[46]

Soviet students are also admitted to Lumumba (1) to help the foreign students learn Russian and adjust to Soviet life; (2) to forestall
criticism that the university was a mechanism for segregating Third
World students; and (3) to learn about Third World countries and particularly their languages.[47] In the early years, only 10 percent of the
student body was Soviet, but that number rose to 25 percent by 1970 and
33 percent by 1980. According to Rubinstein, the increased percentage
of Soviet students is probably related to the adjustment task, which can
be difficult and time-consuming.[48] Another reason for the increase in
Soviet students may be the growing demand for Third World specialists,
given the heightened Soviet interest in the Third World over the past
two decades.

Craig Whitney states that Soviets share dormitories with incoming
foreigners only during the first preparatory year. The foreigners learn
Russian and the Soviets concentrate on learning their roommate's
tongue.[49] After the first intensive year of language studies, the

Soviets remain in the program and follow one of the curricula designed for the country of their specialization.

Whether a Soviet student must remain "married" to his first-year roommate and that foreigner's language and curriculum is unclear. Perhaps a Soviet student, once he has studied the language, can select any of a number of specialties tailored to his chosen country's problems. At any rate, he is likely to develop an intimate knowledge of some aspect of that country's economy and industry.[50]

Table 7 compares a Lumumba University engineering curriculum with the engineering curriculum of a regular Soviet *vuz*. Besides the more practical orientation mentioned earlier, the program is noticeably freer of Marxism-Leninism and other such "social science" courses.[51] University administrators are sensitive to charges that the school is an indoctrination and training center for leftist subversives and terrorists. For example, in a 1980 interview with Whitney, Vladimir F. Stanis, the rector, complained:

> It's unfair to call us a school run by the KGB. There has been much slander about our university. The Voice of America last April broadcast a biography of Carlos, the well-known international terrorist, with the claim that he "got his training at the so-called Patrice Lumumba University, a well-known organ of the KGB," or words to that effect. Well, Carlos did study here. He was expelled after the first year. He failed his courses in 1968. You get such people.[52]

The curricula of the faculty of economics and law at Lumumba retain courses in political economy and philosophy, and the Marxist-Leninist view of the international scene is almost certainly a part of law and history studies.[53] Indeed, Stanis said in the same interview that "We are working for the Soviet Government, with 16 million rubles [$24 million] a year in Soviet Government funds. What would you expect --that we'd teach people to be anticommunist?"[54]

Instruction at Lumumba, because of the individualized curricula, must be painstakingly geared to each student. In 1980, the student-teacher ratio in all six faculties was reportedly five to one, unusually low for an educational system where large lecture halls are the

Table 7

ENGINEERING CURRICULA OF LUMUMBA UNIVERSITY AND
A STANDARD SOVIET ENGINEERING SCHOOL

Lumumba University (Four-year curriculum after year at preparatory faculty)		Standard *Vuz* (Five-year curriculum)	
Subject	Hours	Subject	Hours
Construction fundamentals	114	CPSU history	100
Construction economics	64	Political economy	110
Technology of construction production	114	Marxist-Leninist philosophy	70
Russian for foreigners	164	Fundamentals of scientific communism	70
Higher mathematics	372	Physical education	140
General chemistry	118	Construction economics	70
Descriptive geometry	100	Technology and organization of construction production	112
Mechanical and free-hand drawing	114	Foreign languages	210
Organization and planning of construction	90	Higher mathematics	422
Physics	276	Chemistry	140
Theoretical mechanics	152	Descriptive geometry; mechanical & free-hand drawing	178
Engineering geodesy	82		
Building materials	114	Organization & planning of construction	98
Material resistance; tension fundamentals; plasticity theory	214	Physics	261
		Theoretical mechanics	173
Basic thermotechnics; gas, heat supply; ventilation & air conditioning	82	Engineering geodesy	105
		Building materials	105
Metal technology; welding	82	Material resistance; tension; plasticity theory	213
Construction machinery, including components	114	General thermotechnics; gas, heat supply; ventilation	70
Construction mechanics	202	Metal technology; welding	72
Electrical engineering; electricity for construction	90	Construction machinery, including components	106
Industrial and civil architecture	142	Construction mechanics	220
		Electrical engineering	88
Hydraulics and hydraulic machinery	72	Industrial & civil architecture	221
Water supply and drainage	42	Hydraulics; water supply and drainage	72
Hydrotechnical construction	64		
Engineering geology	54	Engineering geology	56
Mechanics of soil and foundations	82	Mechanics of soil & foundations	98
Testing of construction	48	Testing of construction	42
Computer mathematics; probability theory	56	Computer technology & engineering; economic accounting	42
Production technology of reinforced concrete structures	64	Fundamentals of automation; automation of construction industry processes	42

Table 7 (Cont'd)

Reinforced concrete and stone construction	164	Reinforced concrete and stone construction	168
Wood and plastics construction	48	Wood & synthetic materials construction	84
Metal construction	114	Metal construction	112
		Safety & fire prevention techniques	42
		Courses required by *vuz* council	98
Total hours	3608	Total hours	4210

SOURCE: Seymour M. Rosen, *The Development of Peoples' Friendship University in Moscow*, U.S. Department of Health, Education, and Welfare, (OE)72-132, 1972, pp. 6-7. The Lumumba University curriculum appeared in *Universitet druzhby narodov imeni Patrisa Lumumby--spravochnik*, Moscow, 1967. This official handbook contains curricula for specializations taught at Lumumba University. The standard Soviet engineering school curriculum, approved by the USSR Ministry of Higher and Specialized Secondary Education in 1965, is still in use.

norm.[55] An Indonesian student commented as follows on the value of the teaching methods:

> In the evenings the teachers and their assistants gave consultations and all other possible help to those who needed it. . . . In spite of our systematic studies many still found it difficult to read Russian textbooks. The professors and their assistants therefore went over all the old material, stressing the basic points as they went along. We were given every help in preparing for our exams. We derived a great deal of confidence from the individual attention given to each one of us, and what we failed to grasp was explained again and again.[56]

The academic credentials of the teaching staff are apparently quite good, the result of a concerted effort to strengthen the faculty by bringing in teachers with advanced degrees.[57] Thus, the 1980 staff boasted 620 graduate degrees, including 134 professors and doctors of science.[58]

The university presently has two campuses, one near the Donskoy Monastery in central Moscow and a second under construction since about

1970 in a southwestern suburb.[59] Originally scheduled for completion between 1974 and 1976, some of the facilities were already in use in 1971. However, construction imperatives for the Moscow Olympics caused this schedule to slip, and by 1980 the new campus had still not been finished.[60]

According to university officials, the new facilities will include individual buildings for each academic faculty, a museum, more than 200 workshops and laboratories, a computer center, a clinic for medical students, experimental farm plots, dormitory rooms for 4200 students, a campus club, and a 5000-seat stadium.[61]

What value do Soviet students derive from this institution designed and run for foreign students? As mentioned earlier, about one-third of the present student body is made up of Soviets. In addition, perhaps two-thirds of the school's graduate students are Soviet.[62] Besides helping the foreigners to adjust to Soviet life, these young people receive valuable professional training. Upon graduation, they "become useful to the Soviet Government for work in the Soviet economy generally and in underdeveloped areas, both within and outside the USSR."[63]

In other words, Lumumba may be an excellent training ground for Soviet specialists on the Third World. It may also provide its Soviet graduates with unusual insights into the problems of ethnic minorities in the Central Asian republics of their own country.

However, Soviet students may not be learning as much as they should from their contacts with Third World students, particularly blacks. Sakharov graphically describes the poor, sometimes violent treatment of Africans studying in Moscow.[64] A black student at Lumumba put it more mildly:

> England is a former colonial power. They know what Africans are like, and so do Americans. But the Soviets never had contacts with Africans. This sometimes leads to things that are signs of lack of understanding and can take on the appearance of racism.[65]

Whether racist attitudes affect the learning experience of Soviets at Lumumba is difficult to judge without many firsthand contacts with program graduates.[66] In any case, it seems likely that hostility among segments of the student body would prevent a thorough, mutual understanding of the languages, nationalities, and cultures involved.

Academy of Sciences Institutes

Graduate studies toward a candidate or doctoral degree may be pursued at the institutes of the Academy of Sciences of the USSR. The following are the most important institutes offering such programs in foreign affairs:[67]

Institute of World Economy and International Relations

Institute of the USA and Canada

Institute of Oriental Studies

Institute of Latin America

Institute of the International Worker Movement

Institute of Economics of the World Socialist System

Institute of Africa

Institute of the Far East

A student admitted to IMEMO for graduate studies follows a much different path from that followed by his counterpart in the United States. Instead of attending regular classes, completing requirements, passing general (comprehensive) examinations, and then embarking on dissertation research, the Soviet student probably begins to plan his dissertation right away under the guidance of a *nauchnyy rukovoditel'* (major professor).

After planning his dissertation, the student engages mainly in independent study, although he attends periodic lectures and seminars given by both in-house specialists and outside experts. While conducting his research, he also works at the institute, perhaps as an assistant to his major professor. At some time before graduating, he takes general examinations and when finished with his dissertation, defends it before a two- or three-man panel. If successful, he is then awarded the degree and tital of *kandidat* or *doktor nauk* (candidate or doctor of sciences).[68]

The *nauchnyy rukovoditel'* plays a key role in the academic career of a Soviet graduate student. Without the sponsorship of an in-house adviser, a young man or woman would not be invited to join an institute like IMEMO. Once there, the *aspirant* or graduate student depends on his *rukovoditel'* for support within the institute's bureaucracy as well as for scholarly advice. Loren Graham tells of a situation in which an *aspirant*'s major professor died while the young man was completing his dissertation. Without his mentor's support, the student had a difficult time maintaining his position in the institute.

An *aspirant* also depends on his *rukovoditel'* for interesting work that will give him good experience for his future career. In short, the relationship between major professor and graduate student can be close and personal. To the student, it can be a major means to success in his profession.

Besides gaining the sponsorship of a mentor, a student must pass several hurdles before being admitted to an institute. After a preliminary interview with his *nauchnyy rukovoditel'*, the results of the interview, character references, academic records, and other credentials are submitted to the equivalent of an admissions office in the institute. According to Mark Kuchment, a tug-of-war may ensue at this point. The *rukovoditel'* may want the student, but the admissions office may insist that his other papers be in perfect order.[69] Depending on the institute, he may need a recommendation from the communist party or, in a few cases, a security clearance.[70] Only when the bureaucratic process is over is the applicant ordered to appear for entrance examinations.

Galina Orionova recounts that her entrance examination at IUSAC was oral and covered such material as the amendments to the U.S. Constitution, the role of the Peace Corps, and CPSU history.[71] At other institutes, perhaps those more established than IUSAC was when Orionova applied, entrance examinations cover three basic areas: Marxism and CPSU history, a foreign language, and the specialty that the applicant intends to pursue.

Kuchment recalls that the Academy of Sciences institutes sometimes do not themselves administer entrance examinations in Marxism and CPSU history but will instead send applicants to the Academy of Social

Sciences of the CPSU Central Committee for the examinations. Also,
whether or not an institute administers examinations in foreign languages seems to depend on its size. The larger institutes give their
own examinations; the smaller send their applicants elsewhere. Thus,
an applicant may take only the examination in his specialty at the
institute to which he is applying.

The foreign language examination may have both written and oral
parts. The other two examinations are oral and take place before a
commission. Some questions may be asked on the spot, but usually
candidates are given a list of questions and an hour in which to orga-
nize a written outline of their replies. The examination itself may
take only 45 minutes. Apparently there are no strict time limits, and
the format depends largely on the whim of the examiners.[72]

Once admitted to an institute, an *aspirant* begins working for his
nauchnyy rukovoditel', researching his dissertation, and preparing for
his general examinations (*kandidatskiy minimum*). He prepares for generals by attending seminars at the institute.

The Marxist philosophy seminars are usually compulsory and meet
every week. If a student fails to attend Marxism seminars, both he and
his *nauchnyy rukovoditel'* look bad. The foreign language seminars also
meet weekly, but attendance is not compulsory. If a student feels his
knowledge of a foreign language is good enough to pass the generals, he
need not attend.

Seminars in the student's field of specialization are organized on
a periodic basis. Although attendance is not compulsory, students are
evidently wise to attend such activities. Kuchment notes that special
seminars and conferences in his own department provided good opportunities to make contacts, air research results, and get reactions to ongo-
ing work.

A student may schedule his generals whenever he feels ready to take
them. Usually he must pass them within three years, and before he
writes his dissertation. In some cases, however, the student may take
longer or have completed his dissertation before passing the examinations.

The three-year limit is important for students who are not Moscow
natives and who otherwise do not have jobs that would grant them a

propusk (pass) to live in Moscow. Unless they have ties with a Moscow institute or a *nauchnyy rukovoditel'* in Moscow, these students must return home when their student *propusks* run out and must then complete their dissertations at home-town universities or institutes, a task often made difficult by poor research facilities and lack of contact with specialists in their fields.

The student's need to remain in Moscow to complete his research has been solved, at least in part, by allowing him to be officially associated with a local institution while completing his dissertation work under a *nauchnyy rukovoditel'* at, say, IMEMO. His home institution is then his *vedushchaya organizatsiya* (lead organization) and IMEMO his Moscow base.

Similarly, when an *aspirant* is pursuing a specialization in which his lead organization cannot grant a degree, he must acquire a mentor in an institute with the required expertise and transfer to that institute as a *soiskatel'* or *zaochnyy aspirant*.[73] When he defends his dissertation, the published announcement will note that he completed his work at IMEMO, but that his lead organization was, for example, Kharkov State University.[74]

When a student submits his dissertation for review, it is forwarded to the *golovnaya organizatsiya* (head organization)--the country's most authoritative institution dealing with his specialty. This organization reviews the research and completes a report on it.

The dissertation defense takes place in public before a council of scholars. The student defends his work; then two or three official opponents question him on it. Next, the *golovnaya organizatsiya*'s review is read, and the student answers more questions. Finally, the council takes a private vote. If a clear majority approves the student's work, he is pronounced a *kandidat nauk*. If the result is a tie or a simple majority, he must return in a year to repeat his defense.

The student may be declared a *kandidat* at his dissertation defense, but the benefits of an advanced degree, such as a salary increase, must wait until the degree is confirmed by the *Vysshaya attestatsionnaya komissiya* (Higher Certification Commission) of the USSR Council of Ministers. This powerful organization can impede a scholar's career by withholding confirmation of his degree indefinitely.[75]

Graduate studies in the USSR are generally less structured than graduate studies in the United States and are considerably less structured than Soviet primary and secondary education.[76] In the Soviet system of graduate education, the dissertation and publishing are emphasized much more than course work and examinations. To receive his degree, an *aspirant* at an Academy of Sciences institute, for example, must publish at least two articles in major journals before he completes his dissertation.

Oded Eran notes that institutions like the Academy institutes, originally devoted to teaching and training, became increasingly involved in research during the Brezhnev period. Such active research programs no doubt provide graduate students with better opportunities to gain experience and make contacts. In addition, expanding lines of communication among institutes—both formal and informal—help students to establish themselves in the network of Soviet foreign policy research.[77]

No matter how well-established in Moscow, however, and how excellent their education, most young Soviet foreign area specialists lack an important facet of training—direct exposure to the country of their specialization. A Soviet student would not routinely have the opportunity to live in a foreign country and study at a foreign university. Such a lack of experience abroad could seriously handicap an aspiring internationalist, preventing him from developing and maintaining spoken language fluency and limiting his understanding of his chosen field.

To compensate for this lack of firsthand experience, the Soviets have developed a special system of practical training. Known as the *praktika*, this training program sends students from prestigious institutions like MGIMO and the Academy of Sciences institutes to countries as diverse as the United States and North Yemen. There they work in embassies and other Soviet missions, performing whatever tasks are assigned to them and perhaps also conducting dissertation research.

Dr. Steven Grant, who is well acquainted with the training of Soviet Americanists, said in an interview that the Soviet embassy in Washington and UN mission in New York apparently hold a number of positions open for such students and routinely rent living quarters for them. He did not know, however, whether the student specialists are required to work regular hours at the embassy or mission. It was his impression that they spend as much time on their own research as they do on a job.

Vladimir Sakharov's experience as a MGIMO probationer was somewhat different. He was sent to North Yemen on a routine six-month *praktika* and ended up serving for that period as acting Soviet consul in Hodeida. As such, he held an extremely responsible position and performed many tasks that would usually be assigned to a more senior diplomat.[78]

Thus, the Soviets have apparently found a means of exposing the trusted among their young foreign area specialists to life abroad. This type of practical training could very well make up for the isolation of international studies in the USSR--at least for a select few. For the others, however, the isolation could pose a serious problem, perhaps accounting for the striking misconceptions that westerners have encountered among some of the best-trained Soviet foreign area specialists. Language fluency and knowledge of details would not have been sufficient for them to develop a real understanding of the workings of foreign societies and cultures.[79]

Other Degree Programs

Other degree programs for Soviet foreign area specialists are offered at universities and at institutes attached to ministries other than the Ministry of Foreign Affairs, MGIMO's parent body. Moscow State University, for example, boasts an Institute of the Countries of Asia and Africa; the Ministry of Foreign Trade has an Institute of Foreign Trade; and the Ministry of Defense has a Military Institute training linguists. Moscow State University and the Military Institute are the focus of this section.

Moscow State University and the Institute of the Countries of Asia and Africa. According to Blair Ruble, the Institute of the Countries of Asia and Africa is basically the Eastern Faculty of MGU. It was originally designed to be a research affiliate of the university as well as a teaching institution, but during the 20 years since its founding, the teaching function has taken precedence.[80]

The institute offers both graduate and undergraduate degrees. The undergraduate programs last six years and include a year of *praktika* abroad.[81] The 17 disciplines available during the 1977-1978 school year include Arabic philology; Iranian philology; Indian philology; Chinese philology; Turkish philology; the philologies of the countries of Southeast Asia, Korea, and Mongolia; Japanese philology; West European languages; history of Asian and African literature; African philology; history of the Near and Middle East; history of the Far East and Southeast Asia; history of China; history of Southern Asia; social and political development of Asia and Africa; economics and economic geography of Asia and Africa; and international economic relations.[82]

A student who majors in an eastern language studies the history, ethnography, geography, and economy of his chosen country as well as theoretical linguistics, language, and literature. Depending on his specialization, the student may take courses as exotic as the Teheran dialect of Persian, systems of tenses in the modern Arabic language, history of the Tamil culture of Sri Lanka, or the Kenyan novel--problems of genre.[83]

Despite the variety of course offerings, the language curricula in particular seem designed to produce literature specialists rather than linguists with good conversational ability. Indeed, institute professors who publish in *Vestnik Moskovskogo universiteta* (Moscow University Herald) generally concentrate on literary themes.[84]

Students of economics seem to receive more pragmatic training. They study statistics, accounting, finance, international economics, and planning and programming of the economic development of the countries of Asia and Africa.[85] In addition, they study the history, economy, geography, and government of their chosen area, as well as the socioeconomic aspect of the developing countries and the UN and international law and international economic agreements.[86]

The Institute of the Countries of Asia and Africa has an interesting *praktika* system. In a student's fourth semester in the program, he is sent to the southern republics of the USSR and also to Leningrad and Tartu, Estonia, where the university has a large and ancient manuscript collection. The student uses this trip to study Eastern architecture, art, and manuscripts. In his sixth semester, he spends three weeks in the archives and libraries of Moscow, familiarizing himself with available materials and doing research.

The translation *praktika* takes place in the program's fifth year, when students spend nine weeks working in organizations that generally hire graduates of the institute. According to the MGU catalogue, these include TASS, Novosti, and the State Committee for Economic Relations with Foreign Countries (GKES).[87] This *praktika* seems to be basically an internship during which the organizations try out and train prospective employees.

Finally, the language *praktika* abroad takes place during the program's final year. For 34 weeks, the students are assigned to work abroad in higher educational institutions or as translators. Given the institute's curriculum, many of these students are probably sent to Third World countries.[88]

We know little about the institute's admissions procedure or its teaching staff. The faculty names that appear in the MGU catalogue are not particularly exotic. Many, in fact, seem to be of Russian, Ukrainian, and Armenian extraction. The cadre of Central Asians that might be expected does not, in short, seem to exist--unless, of course, such individuals are lost in the large group of anonymous instructors.

The Military Institute. The Military Institute (*Voyennyy institut*) of the Ministry of Defense, an example of a ministry-sponsored higher educational institution, trains military translator-researchers, foreign language teachers, political workers with knowledge of foreign languages, and lawyers for the armed services. Founded in Moscow in 1942, it was called the Military Institute of Foreign Languages. After acquiring a faculty of military jurisprudence in 1974, it became known simply as the Military Institute.[89]

In a 1980 interview, Colonel-General M. Tankayev, the institute's director, discussed the career paths of the institute's graduates. He recalled that military interpreters had played a vital role in World War II and afterwards at the international military tribunals in Nuremberg and Tokyo. Later, he continued, many had become excellent teachers.

Tankayev gave the example of Doctor of Sciences, Professor, Colonel Gennadiy Nikolayevich Khvatkov. Khvatkov had served as a sergeant during World War II and afterwards entered the institute to become a translator. He returned to the ranks for a while, then continued his studies. Now, according to Tankayev, he chairs a department (*kafedra*) at the institute.[90]

After five years of study, Tankayev said, an institute graduate is first of all an officer, trained to serve in his country's armed forces. Next, he is a well-trained specialist. For example, translator-researchers must know two foreign languages as well as the history and culture of the peoples who speak those languages. Furthermore, as researchers they must be able to respond to any request for information and prepare reports independently.[91]

We have scant information about the institute's curriculum. The *Soviet Military Encyclopedia* states that undergraduate students go through a probationary period in the ranks, spend time on the *praktika*, and get experience as translators. Specific course work is not described. The institute also accepts graduate students in three areas of research: social science (that is, political studies), philology, and military theory.[92]

More is known about the institute's facilities than about its curriculum. Tankayev boasted that the school has the latest in audio equipment, including ten specialized language laboratories, a closed-circuit television system, radio station, computer center, 500,000-volume library, and hundreds of audiovisual aids, including films and tapes. Outside the academic sphere, the school has two gymnasiums, a stadium, shooting range, and playing fields. Tankayev also said that the institute's teaching staff includes 129 doctors and candidates of science and 62 professors and assistant professors (*dotsenty*).[93]

The institute accepts applications from both civilians and servicemen, 17 to 21 years of age. The former apply to their local military commission (recruiting station) and the latter to their commanding officer. Entrance examinations for all departments include Russian language and literature (written and oral), USSR history (oral), and a foreign language (oral).[94]

Tankayev was quite blunt about the type of students admitted to the *Voyennyy institut*: "We have no place for "C" students. Applicants must be physically and mentally strong, idealistic, and perfect students in order to pass our entrance exams."[95]

Kamkov and Konoplyanik admonish hopeful applications to higher military schools to start preparing for the admissions process two to three years *before* submitting an application. They say that two to three years is the minimum required, because experience shows that successful applicants need 2000 to 3000 hours of study time to pass the examinations.[96]

Lacking close contacts with military school graduates, we could not confirm the need for such rigorous preparation. Obviously, the entrance requirements described by Kamkov and Konoplyanik contrast markedly with those described in emigre reports for entrance into prestigious nonmilitary institutes. If, as implied in Tankayev's statement about admissions and Kamkov and Konoplyanik's advice, *blat* plays less of a role at military *vuzy* than at MGIMO or Academy of Sciences institutes, good students may have a greater chance of gaining entry into prestigious military schools without the help of family influence.[97]

The *Voyennyy institut* is the only higher military school that must require an entrance examination in a foreign language.[98] An applicant's spoken knowledge of the language must include the ability to understand foreign speech, answer questions, and converse on subjects that are standard in the high school curriculum. He must be able to read and translate orally, with the help of a dictionary, at the rate of 1100 words an hour. Finally, he must have correct pronunciation and intonation and know the rules of grammar of the language.[99]

Table 8 lists the study program for the institute's English language examination. Clearly, applicants are expected to have a thorough knowledge of grammatical theory. Whether such thoroughness applies to conversational ability in English is open to question. Dunstan points out, however, that the audio-lingual approach used in the special language schools is unusual for the Soviet school system as a whole.[100]

Table 8

STUDY PROGRAM FOR ENGLISH LANGUAGE ENTRANCE EXAMINATION
VOYENNYY INSTITUT

I. Morphology

1. Article. General understanding of the uses of the article.

2. Noun. Formation of the plural. The possessive form. Preposition/noun combinations expressing the same meanings as the cases in Russian.

3. Adjective. Formation of the comparative (general rules and exceptions).

4. Numbers. Ordinal and cardinal numbers.

5. Pronouns. Personal, possessive, indefinite, interrogative, relative, demonstrative.

6. Verb. Personal forms of the verb. Use of the verbs have, be, do, should, would, as independent and auxiliary verbs. Use of the verb be as a linking verb. Use of the verbs be and have as modal verbs. Auxiliary verbs shall, will. Modal verbs can, may, must. "Regular" verbs in the past indefinite and past participle that are formed with the suffix -ed; and the "irregulars" go-went-gone, write-wrote-written. System of verb tenses, including indefinite, continuous, and perfect in the active voice. Formation of the passive voice. Use of verbs in the present, past, future indefinite tense (passive voice); present, past continuous tense (passive voice); present, past perfect tense (passive voice). Imperative mood. Impersonal verb forms: infinitive, past and present participles, gerunds (simple forms). Their functions in a sentence.

7. Adverb. The most common adverbs. Levels of comparison of adverbs.

8. Preposition. The most common prepositions.

9. Conjunction. The most common coordinating and subordinating conjunctions.

10. Word formation. The basic ways of forming nouns, adjectives, verbs, adverbs. The most important suffixes and prefixes.

II. Syntax

1. The simple sentence. Unextended and extended sentences. Main parts of the sentence. Ways of expressing the subject. Types of predicate (simple verbal, predicate adjective, predicate noun). Secondary parts of the sentence. Word order in declaratory, interrogatory, and negative sentences.

2. Compound and compound-complex sentences. The most common type of subordinate clauses.

SOURCE: I. A. Kamkov and V. M. Konoplyanik, *Voyennyye akademii i uchilishcha* (Military Academies and Schools), Moscow, Voyenizdat, 1974, pp. 278-279.

Thus, we would not be surprised if the competence of an institute applicant lay in the field of grammatical theory.

The *Voyennyy institut* is the only higher school attached to the
Ministry of Defense that trains full-time foreign affairs specialists.
The institute's graduates--linguists and researchers in the interna-
tional field--are often assigned to military intelligence (that is, the
Main Intelligence Administration, or GRU).[101] They differ from the
double area specialists who, say, started out in the Strategic Rocket
Forces (SRF) but ended up writing about arms control at IMEMO. Such
specialists are our next subject of discussion.

MGU and the Double Area Specialists

In 1979, five percent of Soviet economic technicians in Third World
countries were agronomists, and six percent were geologists. These per-
centages represent about 1650 agronomists and 1980 geologists.[102] This
section examines the training of such specialists in the agronomy and
geology programs at Moscow State University.

We chose to examine MGU both because we have the best knowledge of
its course schedule and because it is the USSR's most prestigious university, a place to which good students aspire. Also, because it is located in the capital, its graduates may be more likely to find work in
organizations that would place them abroad or use them for jobs requiring foreign contact. Finally, because of the standardized curricula in
the Soviet educational system, the MGU courses probably reflect what is
offered elsewhere in the USSR.

Special institutes also train agronomists and geologists for Third
World service. The agriculture faculty of Lumumba University may be
one such program. The students in the MGU agronomy and geology programs, however, are trained primarily in those two disciplines. We try
to determine their suitability for work outside the USSR, their language
training, and their knowledge of foreign countries, particularly the
Third World.

In the agronomy program at Moscow State University, the soil science faculty trains soil scientist-agrochemists in nine specialties,
none of which is specifically oriented toward conditions outside the

USSR. Several of the specialties under the soil science faculty, however, offer individual "international" courses. In addition, each student must take as general requirements six semesters of English and one class each in world geology and world geography.[103]

A student specializing in the origin of soils will take a course in soils of the world. This course will tell him about the basic soil types of various countries. It will also provide him with the latest information about soil covers worldwide and familiarize him with the most modern world soil maps.[104]

The soil geography specialty offers four such international courses, including applications of aerial photography in soil science, soil cartography, soil coverings of foreign countries, and contemporary problems of soil geography. In the photography course, the students learn to identify soil types from aerial photos of different parts of the world.[105]

In the cartography course, they learn to use mapping instruments and to read soil maps of the USSR and the world. In the foreign soil coverings course, they concentrate on tropical, subtropical, arctic, and tundra regions, learning the soil resources of the world and their use in agriculture. In the soil geography course, they analyze the soil resources of the world and the prospects for expanding agricultural activity while population growth continues.[106]

The last specialty that provides an international orientation is agrochemistry. The course in fundamentals of microfertilization studies the use of trace elements in foreign agriculture. The course in agrometeorology studies the effect of climate on agriculture in various countries and what can be done in certain cases to ameliorate that effect.[107]

The geology and geochemistry of oil and gas deposits is the only specialty in MGU's geology faculty offering an international course. This course, the oil- and gas-bearing deposits of foreign countries, covers the distribution, geologic formation, and reserves of such deposits.[108]

Despite this paucity of specifically foreign-oriented classes, however, the course work of the geology faculty as a whole seems much more generalized to world conditions than that in the soil science faculty. In other words, while soil science courses appear to deal mainly with soil conditions in the USSR, the gas exploration course covers not only the USSR but gas exploration worldwide.

The soil science and geology faculties differ also in their foreign language requirements. Soil science majors are required to study English for six semesters. Geology majors are also required to study a foreign language for six semesters, but they may choose from any of the languages offered in the department of foreign languages for the natural science faculties.[109] This choice means, presumably, that they have a chance to study more unusual languages than English.

Soil scientists most likely learn English so as to follow their specialty in foreign journals. The geologists, although probably just as interested in foreign developments in their field, may want the chance to acquire a language that would help them to work abroad outside of English-speaking areas.

We know of no special admissions procedures for these two faculties.[110] Likewise, we have little information about their teaching staffs and facilities.

Each faculty offers some course work that could help students perform effectively as economic technicians on aid projects in the Third World. The programs include three years of language study, and individual specialties within the programs—soil geography and agrochemistry—provide their students with three or four foreign-oriented courses. However, the number of such courses is small, and we would hesitate to conclude that their impact was important. The students' foreign language knowledge is probably their greatest asset in terms of employment abroad.

Outside of agronomy and geology, other interesting double area specialists are beginning to emerge in the Soviet system. Legvold recounts, for example, that in recent years IMEMO and IUSAC have attracted good students from the Bauman Higher Technical School in Moscow.[111] Bauman, one of the best engineering schools in the USSR,[112] trains students in the applied sciences. According to Legvold, IMEMO and IUSAC teach the Bauman graduates social sciences. The resulting

double area specialists become experts in such topics as western methods of applying computers to management. Other informal ways of drawing scientists, engineers, and others into the Soviet foreign affairs
field are probably also used.

Professional Schools

The professional schools of the Ministry of Defense, Ministry of
Foreign Affairs, communist party, and KGB represent some "formal" ways
of training double area specialists. These schools may not always
award degrees, but they offer opportunities for their students to gain
extra qualifications for moving up the career ladder.

Soviet military men who have become specialists on foreign, especially U.S., defense policy often have done so at the Defense Ministry's
General Staff Academy. The academy, which is located in Moscow, is the
premier institution offering advanced military training to senior military officers. Its international program includes courses on foreign
military doctrines, courses comparing Soviet and western military-
economic potentials, and foreign language courses. Students are expected to utilize their classroom experience in research projects, for
the academy is a major center for the study of military problems, both
applied and theoretical.[113]

Because the General Staff Academy is closed to westerners, our
knowledge of its program, staff, and graduates is limited. Nevertheless, western visitors to IMEMO and IUSAC have received a glimpse of
the expertise on foreign military theory that is available to academy
students thanks to the presence in these two institutes of academy faculty. Since the late 1960s, academy specialists on foreign as well as
Soviet military theory have also been teaching at IMEMO and IUSAC.[114]

The Diplomatic Academy of the Ministry of Foreign Affairs is a
functional equivalent of the U.S. Foreign Service Institute. Kaznacheev regarded its graduates of 20 years ago with some disdain, re-
calling that they were often party hacks who were trying to further
their careers in the diplomatic service:

> They usually have little knowledge of foreign affairs and
> no knowledge of foreign languages. Even after the

two-year course in the school, and day and night language
training, many of them can't be considered to be quite
ready for their future posts abroad. When such a fellow
comes here as the Second Secretary or the First Secretary, he is still unable to put two words in English together, and it takes him almost two years to get an in-
sight into local politics.[115]

Kaznacheev's description somewhat misrepresents the academy's purpose. Triska and Finley point out that the two-year course at the
Diplomatic Academy is a necessary step for career foreign service officers before they can be promoted to senior diplomatic rank.[116] Although Triska and Finley agree that the Diplomatic Academy trains party
officials for diplomatic careers, they do not suggest that this is its
main purpose.

Furthermore, fewer poorly trained *apparatchiki* are to be found in
the diplomatic corps now because fewer exist. The educational level of
party members is generally rising, and even party members seem unable
to reach high positions without advanced degrees. The highest posi-
tions--those in the Central Committee departments--are held by people
who not only have advanced degrees, but also postgraduate training at a
party school. In the foreign affairs field, such advanced training is
provided by the Central Committee's Academy of Social Sciences.

The Academy of Social Sciences in Moscow offers several fields of
specialization oriented toward international work. These include economics and politics of foreign countries, international law, international relations, general history of Russian and western philosophy, and
foreign languages. Graduates of the program staff the Central Committee
departments, institutions of higher learning, research institutes, and
prestigious journals.[117]

Applicants to the Academy must be less than 40 years old and party
members with at least five years' standing. They must also have higher
education, experience in party work, and some capability for research.
Finally, they must pass competitive entrance examinations in their specialty, Marxism-Leninism, and a foreign language.[118]

This system of advanced party training seems to produce well-
qualified foreign affairs specialists, albeit ones with a straightforward

"socialist orientation." This orientation is to be expected, since their first duties are as party theoreticians. However, strict doctrinal guidelines and lack of experience outside the Soviet system may ultimately limit the sophistication that any party-trained specialists might develop. As Triska and Finley put it, "this anonymous man who influences Soviet foreign policy by providing information to his superiors and implementing their directives today possesses a rich substantive sophistication constrained within a simple and rigid Party-given structure of values and priorities."[119] Such rigidity, in turn, tends to produce distortions in the information flow between staff and leadership as specialists shape messages to conform to what leaders want to hear.[120]

The KGB's school for advanced training, the Higher Intelligence School, is located at Belyye Stolby, near Moscow. It offers a two-year postgraduate program for personnel who will work in the Main Directorate of Foreign Intelligence, probably as undercover agents around the world.[121] The curriculum includes ciphers, recruitment techniques, arms, communications, sabotage techniques, communist party history, world economics, world communist movements, and law and legal practices.[122]

The curriculum apparently also includes an excellent foreign language program. The school's recruiter told Sakharov that his English would become perfect, with an emphasis on American slang.[123]

The GRU military intelligence also operates a postgraduate program. Located at the Military-Diplomatic Academy, the program is said to be "the key to advancement to responsible positions in military intelligence abroad."[124] The program is open only to commissioned officers who have finished their higher education. Most of the 75 students accepted each year are of Russian nationality. Curriculum course work stresses general political studies, geographic area studies, foreign languages, and espionage techniques.[125]

The Foreign Affairs, Defense, CPSU, KGB, and GRU professional schools are probably only a few of those in the USSR offering advanced training. Most ministries probably also have a similar program to offer career advancement opportunities to their employees. However, comparatively few produce double area specialists in foreign affairs and a ministry's main area. The organizations discussed here, whose missions are at least partly focused abroad, are the most likely to be training double area specialists.

AN ASSESSMENT OF AREA SPECIALIST TRAINING IN THE USSR

This section has examined the training of foreign area specialists in the USSR. It described a range of educational experiences through all stages of the process, from primary school through postgraduate programs. The aspiring specialists fell into two groups: full-scale internationalists, who pursue a foreign affairs career, and double area specialists, who begin by studying science, math, or military affairs, and end up relating this specialty to some foreign interest.

To conclude the section, we assess the education that both of these specialist types receive in the Soviet system, comparing programs with those available in the United States. We also point out areas where we found information lacking and questions deserving further study.

Generally speaking, the most prestigious foreign affairs training is excellent but available only to a select few. Most students accepted for such training apparently are not chosen on the basis of academic excellence alone, although their educational achievement must be high in order to survive the stringent academic standards in the top schools. A small number, however, probably gain admission to prestige institutes on the basis of capability and native intelligence alone.

Graduates of MGIMO, the Academy of Sciences institutes, and the like speak at least one or two foreign languages well. They almost certainly know English and have spent considerable time perfecting either a British or American accent. In addition, their curriculum was probably tailored to important current issues in their fields. A student of the United States, for example, may have taken courses similar to those found in U.S. business schools. Thus, he would be familiar with the workings of international markets, multinational corporations, and other phenomena of the capitalist system.

In short, academic programs in the prestigious institutions have been specifically designed to impart to students a detailed knowledge of world trends. However, the sophistication of that knowledge can be limited by two factors: strict adherence to a Marxist-Leninist viewpoint and lack of contact with the outside world. The Soviets recognize the problem caused by the second factor and have taken steps to remedy it.

The most important of these steps is probably the expanded use of the *praktika* abroad. The Soviet government sets aside positions in embassies and other missions for students of MGIMO, IUSAC, IMEMO, MGU's Institute of the Countries of Asia and Africa, and others. The students thus have an opportunity to live, work, and study abroad, gaining firsthand knowledge of their country of specialization and perfecting their knowledge of its language. The government pays for this training because it is grooming these students for important positions in the foreign affairs field. They probably will serve the government all their lives, and therefore the investment is almost certainly a good one.

A way to overcome the isolation of Soviet students of the Third World has been developed at the Patrice Lumumba Peoples' Friendship University. Soviet students entering Lumumba live for their first year with a student from a developing country, learning his language and customs. Thereafter, the Soviets follow curricula designed expressly to address the problems in their country of specialization. Thus, they obtain a more vivid and practical knowledge of the Third World than that to be gained simply from textbooks and lectures.

In MGU's Institute of the Countries of Asia and Africa during one academic year, students could take courses ranging from the Kenyan novel to the Teheran dialect to the Tamil culture of Sri Lanka. Other schools like MGIMO and the Institute of Foreign Languages probably offer similar variety. Certain universities and institutes in the USSR appear to maintain a range of foreign area courses that would be impossible at most institutions of higher learning in the United States. The costs of staff, facilities, and teaching materials would simply be too high for one university to bear, particularly if the program were uncertain of attracting students.

Another difference between the United States and USSR involves the level of knowledge needed to gain admission to a foreign area training program. The *Voennyy institut* requires a thorough knowledge of English grammar and syntax of students who want to enter its English language faculty. Its U.S. counterpart, the Defense Language Institute at Monterey, requires no knowledge of Russian for entrance, but relies on language aptitude tests to determine which applicants are suited to learning Russian.

This difference may be a function of theories of language teaching in each country, and it may be a function of the level of achievement in foreign language that each country expects of its secondary school graduates. Whether or not the difference is significant depends on the end products of each system. Unfortunately, data for such a comparison are sparse.

Our examination of the double area specialist phenomenon has turned up a range of possible expertise levels. For example, the Moscow University catalogue implies that agronomy and geology majors receive training that would prepare them to work in the Third World; that is, they take some courses with an international orientation, particularly foreign languages.

The six semesters of language study that agronomy and geology students receive at MGU represent more exposure than most agronomy and geology majors get in the United States. However, the purpose of the Soviet language requirement remains unclear. Almost certainly it is intended to help students follow foreign developments in their fields. In addition, it may prepare them for possible service abroad.

We have a much clearer idea of the expertise gained in other double area specialist training programs. For example, graduates of the Bauman Higher Technical School have been going to IMEMO and IUSAC for foreign area studies to become expert in fields such as western computer technology.

The professional schools of the communist party, defense and foreign ministries, and intelligence services also provide training that is unambiguously international in nature. Judging from the high positions that their graduates attain, those schools are performing the mission required of them. We can argue, of course, that the Marxist-Leninist viewpoint and closed Soviet society lessen the sophistication of such double area specialists. However, we cannot dispute that they study foreign languages and international relations systematically, thus adding to their qualifications in other fields.

Several questions deserve further study in this regard. From contacts with Soviet embassy personnel and academic exchange scholars, we have a fairly good impression of the level of competence that they attain at MGIMO, the Academy of Sciences institutes, and other prestigious training grounds. But what of those who travel outside the USSR to areas generally remote from western observation? Economic and military aid personnel in developing countries would be included in this group.

Information on these two types of foreign area specialists is available. However, to obtain it would require extensive contacts with recent emigres from the USSR and with U.S. foreign service personnel, journalists, and businessmen who have observed Soviets working in the Third World.

We also found that quantitative data on the Soviet foreign affairs field are lacking in most regards. Unavailable data include budget figures; numbers of students, teachers, and researchers in institutes; and numbers of professionals in the field as a whole. However, one could gain some insights into the magnitude of the Soviet foreign area effort, for example, by assessing the numbers of articles or dissertations annually published in various branches of the foreign affairs field.

In sum, the training of internationalists in the Soviet system produces some specialists who are clearly equal to the job assigned them. Such specialists are the graduates of prestigious institutions, both those devoted to the international field and those devoted to double areas. However, other specialists, especially in double areas, seem to receive an education with no particular emphasis on foreign affairs. Any preparation they receive for work abroad probably stems from their language training and other course work generalized to apply to the world outside the USSR.

Section II Notes

1. We are indebted to the International Research and Exchanges Board (IREX) for this information.

2. John Dunstan, *Paths to Excellence and the Soviet School*, NFER Publishing Company, Windsor, Berkshire (UK), 1978, p. 92. Our discussion of special language schools is based largely on Dunstan's fine account. Another good source on the subject is Diana E. Bartley, *Soviet Approaches to Bilingual Education*, Center for Curriculum Development, Philadelphia, 1971.

3. Soviet commentators have mentioned careers for special language school graduates ranging from international sleeping car attendants through lab technicians and computer programmers to diplomats. Dunstan, p. 94.

4. Ibid., p. 98.

5. Ibid., p. 96.

6. Ibid.

7. Dunstan's excellent discussion of the prestige factor appears on pp. 98-102. On pp. 101-102, he summarizes his remarks thus: "To regard [the special language school program] as a deliberate piece of social engineering to cater for elitist aspirations is considerably less reasonable than to interpret it as the inadvertent outcome of a policy orientated on the pragmatic goal of providing the labour market with young people specially skilled in a foreign language, which nevertheless furnished a rare opportunity of working the system."

8. Ibid., p. 99.

9. Ibid.

10. E. Polyakova, "Bol'shaya Moskva, Medvedkovo" (Greater Moscow, Medvedkovo District), *Novyy mir*, No. 10, 1967, p. 156; cited in Dunstan, p. 99, and fn 50.

11. Ibid., p. 99.

12. Ibid., pp. 107-108. Dunstan cites a Soviet study of the overloading that occurs in special schools, leading to mental and physical strain on students and more frequent illness. See N. B. Bushanskaya and N. N. Rundal'tseva, "Zabolevayemost' uchashchikhsya shkol s prepodavaniyem ryada predmetov na inostrannom yazyke" (Morbidity of Pupils in Schools Teaching a Number of Subjects in a Foreign Language), *Sovetskoye zdravookhraneniye*, No. 12, 1968, pp. 37-40, cited in Dunstan, fns 30 and 90.

13. Dunstan, p. 103.

14. Otherwise, the curriculum of the special schools is identical to that of ordinary schools. Below is a sample curriculum from Dunstan (p. 104):

Curriculum in RSFSR Foreign Language Schools, 1972–1973

Subject	Periods per Week per Grade									
	1	2	3	4	5	6	7	8	9	10
Russian Language	12	11	10	6	5	4	3	2	–	1
Russian Literature	–	–	–	2	2	2	2	3	4	3
Mathematics	6	6	6	6	6	6	6	5	6	6
History	–	–	–	2	2	2	2	3	4	3
Social Studies	–	–	–	–	–	–	–	–	–	2
Nature Study	–	–	2	–	–	–	–	–	–	–
Geography	–	–	–	–	2	3	2	2	2	–
Biology	–	–	–	–	2	2	2	2	1	2
Physics	–	–	–	–	–	2	2	3	4	5
Astronomy	–	–	–	–	–	–	–	–	–	1
Technical Drawing	–	–	–	–	–	–	1	2	–	–
Chemistry	–	–	–	–	–	–	2	2	3	3
Foreign Language	–	3	3	3	6	6	6	4	4	4
Foreign Literature[a]	–	–	–	–	–	–	–	2	2	2
Art	1	1	1	1	1	1	–	–	–	–
Music and Singing	1	1	1	1	1	1	1	–	–	–
Physical Education	2	2	2	2	2	2	2	2	2	2
Work Training[b]	2	2	2	2	2	2	2	2	2	2
Elementary Military Training	–	–	–	–	–	–	–	–	2	2
Total periods per week	24	26	25	27	31	33	33	34	36	38

[a] In the foreign language.

[b] In grades nine and ten: technical translation or typing in the foreign language.

NOTE: In foreign language lessons in grades two to ten, and if necessary in subjects taught in the foreign language (including technical drawing and typing in grades nine and ten), the class is divided into three groups of ten pupils each.

SOURCE: *Sbornik prikazov i instruktsii Ministerstva prosveshcheniya RSFSR*, No. 11, 1972, pp. 4–5.

15. Dunstan recalls meeting a Soviet teacher of English who was panicked by the request that he teach mathematics in English. Dunstan says that "he had no idea how to explain mathematical procedures in English and desperately needed some textbooks" (p. 107).

16. Ibid., p. 106.

17. See the curriculum listing in note 14. Dunstan's discussion of this problem appears on pp. 106–107.

18. Dunstan, p. 94.

19. Allen H. Kassof, Executive Director of the International Research and Exchanges Board, suggested this term to us. Soviet researchers have also recognized the concept: "The breakdown of the social, natural, and technical sciences is not intended to indicate an opposition between them; it is their interdependence that is important for scientific and technical progress. The interdependence of the sciences is evidenced by the periodic output of scientific workers which goes beyond the framework of their area of specialization." Quoted in Catherine P. Ailes et al., "Summary of Soviet Report on the Training and Utilization of Scientific, Engineering, and Technical Personnel in the USSR" (Draft), Stanford Research Institute, Washington, D.C., July 1979, p. 71.

20. Unfortunately, we have neither the time nor space here to describe exhaustively all of the *vuzy* that train foreign affairs specialists in the USSR. We emphasize MGIMO because its standard is probably matched but not surpassed by other institutes. For an excellent overview of the institutions involved in the field, see Blair A. Ruble, *Soviet Research Institutes Project, Volume I: The Policy Sciences*, United States Information Agency, Office of Research, R-5-81, February 19, 1981. (Hereafter cited as *Soviet Research Institutes Report*.)

21. In the Soviet system, the degree of *doktor* is awarded to senior researchers. For a discussion of the differences between the degree of *doktor* and the Ph.D. in the United States, see note 68, below.

22. Aleksandr Kaznacheev, *Inside a Soviet Embassy*, J. B. Lippincott Co., New York, 1962, p. 29.

23. Vladimir Sakharov, *High Treason*, G. P. Putnam's Sons, New York, 1980, p. 53.

24. Sakharov, p. 67.

25. Ibid., pp. 71-73.

26. Nora Beloff, "Escape from Boredom: A Defector's Story," *Atlantic Monthly*, November 1980, p. 42.

27. Beloff, p. 42. Orionova mentions that she applied for regular graduate studies at the institute, but that its director, Georgiy Arbatov, asked her to take a job instead. He needed the graduate student slots for young men so as to defer them from military service. Orionova was still allowed to work on her graduate degree and earned it in five years. See p. 43.

28. Jan F. Triska and David D. Finley, *Soviet Foreign Policy*, The Macmillan Company, New York, 1968, p. 95.

29. Interview with Robert Legvold.

30. Sakharov, pp. 109, 111.

31. Sakharov, p. 52; and Kaznacheev, p. 28.

32. See, for example, Sakharov, p. 82, and Kaznacheev, pp. 30-31. Sakharov emphasizes the espionage aspects of his MGIMO training and Kaznacheev the more rigorous academic aspects.

33. Ruble also notes that N. N. Inozemtsev, IMEMO's director, is a MGIMO alumnus. Ruble says that MGIMO has recently "become a 'feeder' school for graduate studies at IMEMO and, assuming that old school ties make a difference in the USSR, it is likely that the institute will remain a primary training ground for Moscow's elite." *Soviet Research Institutes Report*, p. 400.

34. Ibid.

35. Seymour M. Rosen, *Soviet Programs in International Education*, U.S. Department of Health, Education, and Welfare, (OE)75-19115, November 1974, p. 24.

36. Sakharov, p. 89. Sakharov mentions that graduates of this faculty went on to become high-level Central Committee representatives in Soviet embassies abroad. For more on these representatives, see pp. 110-111.

37. Kaznacheev, p. 31. He also says that language training constitutes about 40 percent of a MGIMO student's program.

38. Sakharov, p. 88.

39. Ibid., p. 85.

40. Kaznacheev, p. 30. Soviet educators have addressed the problem of improving political training methods in all higher educational institutions. See, for example, I. Mareyev, "Chem interesna lektsiya?" (What Makes the Lecture Interesting?), *Kommunist Vooruzhennykh sil*, No. 19, October 1982, pp. 56-62.

41. Sakharov, p. 84. Other sources confirm the Soviets' knowledge of western commercial and business practices. Dr. Steven A. Grant described in an interview the difficulty that Soviet foreign trade officials had arranging for U.S. experts to set up the Kama River Truck Plant. The officials finally called in Soviet management specialists from IUSAC to act as consultants on the project. See also Grant's *Soviet Americanists*, International Communication Agency, Office of Research, R-1-80, February 15, 1980, p. 5, and fn 13; and Oded Eran, *The Mezhdunarodniki--An Assessment of Professional Expertise in the Making of Soviet Foreign Policy*, Turtledove Publishing, Ramat Gan, Israel, 1979, p. 238.

42. Seymour M. Rosen, *The Development of Peoples' Friendship University in Moscow*, U.S. Department of Health, Education, and Welfare, (OE)72-132, 1972, p. 3. (Hereafter cited as *Peoples' Friendship University*.)

43. Ibid. Alvin Rubinstein mentions that the preparatory faculty was eventually supposed to "wither away" as students arrived with better qualifications. However, he says, "Soviet officials now admit that the level of student preparation is not always as high as they would like; indeed, the need for a year of intensive study of the Russian language more than justifies the continuation of the faculty's separate status." See Alvin Z. Rubinstein, "Lumumba University: An Assessment," *Problems of Communism*, November-December 1971, p. 64.

44. *Peoples' Friendship University*, p. 3.

45. Rubinstein, p. 67.

46. *Peoples' Friendship University*, p. 5.

47. Ibid., p. 3.

48. Rubinstein, p. 66.

49. Craig R. Whitney, "Lumumba U: Is It a Soviet Tool?" *New York Times*, January 6, 1980.

50. Interview with Seymour Rosen.

51. "Social science" in the Soviet context generally means Marxist philosophy and other such political or ideological subjects. Only when writing for western audiences do Soviet authors use social science in the western sense. (See quotation in fn 19, above.)

52. Whitney.

53. See *Peoples' Friendship University*, p. 4.

54. Whitney.

55. Ibid.

56. Quoted in *Peoples' Friendship University*, p. 14.

57. Ibid., p. 11.

58. Whitney calls these titles "academically impeccable."

59. Ibid.

60. Ibid., and *Peoples' Friendship University*, p. 1. In Rubinstein's view, "that Moscow believes in the value of the University is evident from the decision to construct new and more impressive quarters for it," p. 69.

61. Ibid., and *Peoples' Friendship University*, p. 1.

62. Ibid., p. 8.

63. Ibid., p. 10.

64. Sakharov, pp. 188-189.

65. Quoted in Whitney. See also Rubinstein, pp. 68-69.

66. The authors had only one such contact, a Soviet specialist on international law who had graduated from Lumumba. He volunteered the information that he disliked Third World people and that his experience at Lumumba had confirmed this dislike.

67. See *Soviet Research Institutes Report*, pp. 379-400.

68. Much of the information presented in this section was obtained in interviews with Seymour Rosen, Robert Legvold, Steven Grant, and Loren Graham. Graham emphasized the point that the *doktor nauk* is not equivalent to the Ph.D. in the United States. The Soviet degree is awarded after years of research and to comparatively few. If a postdoctoral degree existed in the U.S. system, the *doktor nauk* would be its equivalent.

69. We are grateful to Mark Kuchment for his recollections of the admissions process at Academy of Sciences institutes. Kuchment, a graduate of the Academy's Institute of the History of Natural Science and Technology, is now associated with the Russian Research Center at Harvard University.

70. Oded Eran (p. 249) names the Institute of the Far East as one that requires security clearances.

71. Beloff, p. 43.

72. Interview with Kuchment. This informality provides an opportunity for the type of *pro forma* entrance exams that Vladimir Sakharov had at MGIMO. The preexamination screening clearly seems more important than the examinations themselves.

73. *Soiskatel'* (competitor) is the functional equivalent of a U.S. Ph.D. candidate, but the term carries the connotation of a job classification similar to that of a research fellowship. In simple terms, a *soiskatel'* is a graduate student whose official job is to prepare a dissertation defense. *Aspirant*, on the other hand, seems to carry no job connotation. A *zaochnyy aspirant* is a graduate student who studies by correspondence. This process may involve graduate work in Moscow on a part-time basis or at night, or it may literally involve correspondence between a mentor in Moscow and his student elsewhere.

74. Such announcements appear annually in the March issue of *Mirovaya ekonomika i mezhdunarodnyye otnosheniya*, IMEMO's journal. We are grateful to Steven Grant and Mark Kuchment for clarifying the lead organization concept.

75. Interview with Kuchment.

76. Kuchment stresses the informality of the Academy system, noting that the rules can differ drastically for various individuals. The *nauchnyy rukovoditel'* can play a particularly important role in smoothing his protege's progress. He can make it possible for a student to remain in Moscow, for example, even if his three-year residence permit has run out.

77. Eran, pp. 257, 148. Robert Legvold has also noted the phenomenon of expanding communication lines. He mentioned in an interview that he thought that the flow of people and information among institutes would continue to grow, particularly in an informal sense. He said that because the system is bureaucratically rigid, communication is likely to take place informally, as part of an old boy network. Under such circumstances, a student's relationship with a well-placed mentor becomes even more important.

78. Sakharov, pp. 147-176.

79. Gregory Guroff noted that Soviet specialists on the United States "have perhaps the greatest difficulty in appreciating the multiplicity of political and economic power bases in the U.S. . . . They have concentrated on understanding the White House, the Congress, 'big' business and labor 'bosses'. . . . This approach has so permeated Soviet thinking that even those best informed about the U.S. retreat to

cliches when confronted by the complexity and dynamism of the American political system." Gregory Guroff, *Soviet Perceptions of the U.S.: Results of a Surrogate Interview Project*, U.S. Information Agency, Office of Research, M-16-80, June 27, 1980, p. 9.

80. *Soviet Research Institutes Report*, p. 381.

81. Ibid., p. 382.

82. Ibid. See also *Moskovskiy universitet 1977/1978 katalog-spravochnik (gumanitarnyye fakul'tety)* [Moscow University 1977/1978 Catalogue-Handbook (Humanities Faculties)], Izdatel'stvo Moskovskogo universiteta, Moscow, 1977, pp. 456-457. (Hereafter cited as *Moscow U. Catalogue*.)

83. *Moscow U. Catalogue*, pp. 466-469.

84. *Soviet Research Institutes Report*, p. 382.

85. Ibid. *Moscow U. Catalogue*, pp. 474-475.

86. Ibid., pp. 476-477. Economics majors do not seem to spend much time learning the language of their area.

87. Ibid., p. 460. The use of foreign area specialists by TASS, Novosti, and GKES is discussed in greater detail on pp. 77, 82, 84, 108-109, below.

88. Ibid. Martha Brill Olcott points out that the Soviets distinguish between "hard currency" and "soft currency" exchanges in sending students abroad. Students of the Institute of Latin American Studies told her that most of them went on field trips once or twice a year if their area of specialty was covered by a reciprocal currency agreement. Her own experience at the USSR Institute of Ethnography bore out the Soviet students' statement. Trips to the United States, which require hard currency, are more desirable but less frequent. (Personal communication, November 11, 1982.)

89. I. S. Katyshkin, "Voyennyy Institut," *Sovetskaya voyennaya entsiklopediya*, Vol. 2, 1976, p. 267.

90. Interview with M. Tankayev, "Est' takoy institut" (There Is Such an Institute), *Voyennoye znaniye*, No. 7, 1980, p. 12.

91. Ibid., p. 13. According to another source, graduates leave the institute with the rank of lieutenant. See I. A. Kamkov and V. M. Konoplyanik, *Voyennyye akademii i uchilishcha* (Military Academies and Schools), Voyenizdat, Moscow, 1974, p. 48.

92. *Sovetskaya voyennaya entsiklopediya*, Vol. 2, 1976, p. 267.

93. Tankayev, p. 13.

94. Ibid. See also Kamkov and Konoplyanik, p. 48.

95. Tankayev, p. 13.

96. Ibid., pp. 61-62. Kamkov and Konoplyanik refer in this context to actual academic preparation for entrance exams, rather than to the type of regime that Sakharov followed to gain entry into MGIMO (see above, pp. 20-21).

97. This statement may not apply to graduates of the Suvorov and Nakhimov schools, which are high-school-level military academies. Many of the students in these schools are apparently children of ranking military officers. As Suvorov or Nakhimov graduates, they can be admitted to higher military schools without taking entrance examinations. Ibid., p. 96, and Triska and Finley, p. 103.

98. Kamkov and Konoplyanik, p. 95.

99. Ibid., p. 277.

100. Dunstan, p. 103.

101. Harriet Fast Scott and William F. Scott, *The Armed Forces of the USSR*, Westview Press, Boulder, Colorado, 1979, p. 368.

102. *Communist Aid Activities in Non-Communist Less Developed Countries, 1979 and 1954-79*, Central Intelligence Agency, ER 80-10318U, October 1980, pp. 2-3.

103. *Moscow U. Catalogue*, pp. 444, 448, 453.

104. Ibid., p. 456.

105. Ibid., p. 460.

106. Ibid., p. 462.

107. Ibid., p. 471.

108. Ibid., p. 499.

109. Ibid., p. 479.

110. For the general rules of admissions to Soviet universities, see Seymour M. Rosen, *Education in the USSR--Current Status of Higher Education*, Office of Education, Washington, D.C., 1980.

111. Interview with Robert Legvold.

112. Nicholas De Witt, *Education and Professional Employment in the USSR*, National Science Foundation, Washington, D.C., 1961, p. 216.

113. Scott and Scott, pp. 353-354; V. G. Kulikov (ed.), *Akademiya General'nogo shtaba* (The General Staff Academy), Voyenizdat, Moscow, 1976, pp. 194-196, 201, and 203-211.

114. Scott and Scott, p. 355.

115. Kaznacheev, p. 42.

116. Triska and Finley, pp. 98-99.

117. Ibid., p. 93.

118. Ibid. The reader will recall that students applying to the Academy of Sciences institutes sometimes take Marxism-Leninism and foreign language entrance examinations at the Academy of Social Sciences. See pp. 32-33, above.

119. Triska and Finley, p. 94.

120. Gregory Guroff, *Soviet Elite Sources of Information on the U.S.: Availability and Credibility*, United States Information Agency, Office of Research, M-33-80, November 26, 1980, p. 2.

121. Triska and Finley, p. 102; and Sakharov, p. 184.

122. Ibid.

123. Ibid., pp. 184–185.

124. Triska and Finley, p. 103.

125. Ibid.

III. CAREER AND ROLE OF THE SOVIET AREA SPECIALIST

INTRODUCTION

This section details the tasks and roles of Soviet workers trained in foreign language and area studies and working in a wide range of fields in the USSR. As in the preceding section, we examine two types of specialist engaged in international work: the foreign area specialist by training and professional status and the double area specialist described earlier.

Foreign and double area specialists hold numerous and diverse positions in the USSR. Thus, this section takes on the nature of a survey covering all the areas of specialist activity that we discovered during our research.

Unfortunately, the survey method has limitations. In many cases, we have not been able to look beyond the jobs to the qualifications and effectiveness of those who fill them. Thus, although we know that thousands of Soviet military men are working as aid personnel in the Third World, we know neither to what extent they are specially trained to work abroad nor how effective they are in dealing with their clients.

Furthermore, the available data are limited. The Soviets do not publish detailed employment figures in various fields, so we have not been able to provide an accurate impression of the numerical distribution of specialists among relevant academic, government, party and military organizations.

Several trends are worth noting, however. First and most significant, more Soviets, both civilian and military, are serving abroad and gaining exposure for the USSR, especially in the Third World. Second, the level of educational attainment and professional polish that seems to be expected in the diplomatic service and academia is rising.

Finally, as Soviet foreign contacts have increased, the bureaucratic structure of ministries and other agencies has apparently expanded to accommodate the greater demand, and many government agencies now have elaborate structures for handling foreign contacts. Some of

these offices have several missions to fulfill, and all of them require
that their staffs have foreign area expertise.

This section considers ten major areas of specialist activity:
education, research, the media, government agencies, party organizations, the military, intelligence services, missions abroad, commercial enterprises, and international exchange organizations. Where information was available, we describe each area according to its international missions, the agencies that exist to fulfill those missions,
and the role of foreign area specialists employed by the agencies. We
also try to convey an impression of what the individual jobs are like
and what makes some of them more appealing than others to area specialists in the USSR.

EDUCATION

Our preceding discussions of both general foreign area training
and special foreign area training indicates that there are many jobs in
Soviet education for area specialists. Primary schools, secondary
schools, and higher educational institutions all require language, history, geography, and other teachers who know about the world outside
the USSR. This section concentrates on job placement for language
teachers, research in teaching institutions, career development, and
academic exchanges.

Unfortunately, we can supply no exact information about the number of Soviet teachers in the foreign affairs field. Assuming more-or-
less uniform curriculum requirements across the country, however, we
may further assume that every school, whether located in the remotest
village or in the largest city, needs at least one foreign language,
history, and geography teacher.

Considering the fact that there are about 150,000 general education schools alone in the USSR,[1] we may conclude that a large number
of teachers is needed. The Soviet Statistical Yearbook lists 174,000
language teachers, 100,000 geography teachers, and 166,000 history
teachers working in day schools during the 1978-1979 academic year.[2]
These figures do not include those working in night schools, nor do
they include those teaching more than one subject.

Soviet teachers are trained at pedagogical schools, institutes,
and universities, the latter two providing a higher education and the
first providing a complete secondary education. Once graduated, how
are they placed in jobs? Are certain jobs considered more desirable
than others? Must teachers remain where they are placed? A recent
article in *Kommunist*, the official party journal, answers some of
these questions, at least as they apply to foreign language teaching.

In the *Kommunist* article, Z. Verdiyeva, rector of the Azerbay-
dzhan Pedagogical Institute of Foreign Languages, discusses the difficulty that the school's commission for job assignments has in placing
graduates outside large cities. Verdiyeva explains that students often
come to the institute thinking that they are destined for glamorous
jobs as guides and translators. They then must be told that the institute trains only teachers and, basically, teachers destined to work in
rural regions of the republic.[3]

Most applicants, although momentarily taken aback, nevertheless
assert that they are ready for such a life. The difficulty comes five
years later, when they graduate and go before the job assignment commission. By then, according to Verdiyeva, many of the students have
found husbands or jobs in the city and intend to stay there, although
by so doing they are breaking the law.[4]

Verdiyeva described one of. the institute's graduates who had
married only to escape from rural service. As soon as the commission
excused her, she got a divorce. On learning of the divorce, the commission assigned her to a job in a rural area. Thus she did not escape, but Verdiyeva was concerned because the young woman thought that
she could get away with her trick in the first place.[5]

The article condemns *blat*, which affects not the admissions process, but job assignments and the "socially useful labor" expected of
all students, like helping with the potato harvest. Verdiyeva's description of meddling in job assignments is enlightening:

> Sometimes, illegal methods of helping students escape from
> assignments take the form of official requests for them
> from extremely reputable institutions. Understand, this
> student didn't appear to be special either in his studies

or his public life, but suddenly a "paper" arrives, stating that he is an irreplaceable specialist and that an important government establishment cannot wait to get him and only him. We have appealed many times to the party organizations of such institutions to find out what was behind this "official request," only to be told that philoprogenitive parents with the help of equally "sensitive" friends were trying to guarantee the future of their children at the expense of the government.[6]

Verdiyeva attributes the problem to the fact that teaching languages has fallen in popularity among youth to the level of more prosaic occupations like shop attendant or bank clerk. No one takes any time to instill professional pride in the students, and the result is obvious.[7]

Because Verdiyeva's article appeared in *Kommunist*, we may assume that the problems are of some magnitude. However, we also suspect that they are less serious in institutes whose students are not destined for rural service. If a student can stay in a large city when he graduates, he will not necessarily need to expend the influence available to him on finding a safe job or convenient marriage.[8]

According to Steven Grant, most major research on the United States --*amerikanistika* in Soviet parlance--is carried out in four main centers, all located in Moscow. In descending order of importance, these centers are IMEMO, IUSAC, Moscow State University, and the Institute of World History.[9] The first two are directly tasked by the Central Committee departments of the CPSU, a link that Grant considers important in the policymaking context. Furthermore, because their directors seem to be close advisers to the top leadership, the institutes have enjoyed high visibility worldwide.[10]

As noted earlier, MGU's Institute of the Countries of Asia and Africa, designed to be both a research and a teaching institution, has slipped increasingly away from research in recent years. Is this also true of other university research on foreign affairs, particularly as the Academy of Sciences institutes gain prestige?

Grant suggests that if a trend away from research exists, it is neither inevitable nor irreversible. If MGU or another university is

able to carve out an area of expertise in the foreign affairs field,
then it is a research as well as a teaching entity. Such was the case
with MGU's Problem Laboratory on *Amerikanistika*.

Apparently, Grant says, the Ministry of Higher Education decided
to establish the laboratory to counteract the overwhelming influence of
IMEMO and IUSAC.[11] Its director, Professor N. V. Sivachev, found a
research topic receiving inadequate attention from the two institutes,
namely, the history and present status of the U.S. two-party system,
and began to develop expertise on the subject at MGU.[12]

Sivachev's efforts seem to have paid off, at least to judge from
the evidence we see of greater understanding of the U.S. system in the
Soviet media. Grant sees IMEMO and IUSAC researchers benefiting from
their (presumed) association with the university scholars.[13]

However, university research and teaching programs may be hampered
by the tendency of the distinction between research and teaching institutions to become increasingly blurred.[14] As the Academy institutes
become well-established research centers, they may plausibly gain an
advantage over the universities in teaching too, at least in teaching
foreign affairs graduate students. In other words, if a graduate student can find superior research opportunities as well as instruction
at an Academy institute, he may be inclined to choose it over the university. Thus, talented students may gravitate away from MGU to the
Academy institutes.

Students everywhere, including the USSR, use graduate studies to
advance their careers, obtain a raise, and otherwise improve their
standing in the academic and professional communities. In the USSR,
however, according to Mark Kuchment, career advancement through graduate studies depends on where an individual is located in the USSR.[15]

The role of the lead organization in providing provincial students
with a means to complete their *kandidat* degrees once their Moscow residence permits expire was noted in Section II. These students return to
a hometown university or institute, but continue their dissertation research under the guidance of a *nauchnyy rukovoditel'* in Moscow.

Kuchment asserts, however, that this arrangement is not necessary in many cases. If the student is competent and advancing well in his research, his *nauchnyy rukovoditel'* will "take care of him." The *rukovoditel'* may, for example, recommend the student for a job in a Moscow-based organization, at the same time agreeing with the student's future boss that he be given time to finish his dissertation. The future boss can usually be persuaded that the free time allotted is actually a good investment for his organization. Furthermore, the student receives a permanent Moscow resident permit and may remain in Moscow for as long as he wants.

If the student returns to the provinces, according to Kuchment, he need not finish his dissertation and defend it, because even with an incomplete *kandidat* degree he can obtain a post as an assistant professor at his hometown university. He may be content to remain in that position all his life, especially if he has no chance of permanent residence in Moscow.

As Kuchment puts it, the job of assistant professor is comfortable enough for many, so why should they bother to defend a dissertation? However, if a chance came to return to the capital, an individual with an incomplete *kandidat* would probably have to finish his degree to survive in the more competitive Moscow atmosphere.

For at least 20 years, Soviet educators in the foreign affairs field have been participating in academic exchanges with the socialist bloc, western countries, and the developing world. Most foreign area specialists who have gone to western countries have been language teachers; Soviet history and geography teachers would have comparatively little interest in the western social sciences, except for teaching methods and materials. Seymour Rosen notes that this lack of interest "is consistent with Soviet concern to protect prescribed Marxist-Leninist curriculum content from bourgeois or capitalist elements."[16]

Educational exchanges have taken many forms, both bilateral and multilateral. Most bilateral exchanges occur under provisions of scientific, technical, and cultural exchange agreements with individual countries.

The U.S.-USSR "Agreement on Exchanges in the Scientific, Technical, Educational, Cultural and Other Fields" broke down in 1980, after
the Soviet invasion of Afghanistan. Prior to that, however, the United
States and USSR had had a series of two-year agreements since January
1958.[17]

The U.S.-USSR agreement called for exchanges of graduate students
and young researchers, summer exchanges of language teachers, exchanges
of university professors to give lectures and conduct research, and exchanges of delegations to study methodology.[18]

The U.S.-USSR annual language teacher summer exchanges involved an
equal number of Soviets and American language teachers who spent eight
weeks, from around the second week in June until the end of August, in
the United States and USSR, respectively. The Americans studied at
Moscow State University, the Soviets at various universities around the
United States. In 1976, the Soviets went to the University of Cali-
fornia at Los Angeles, and in 1977, the State University of New York in
Buffalo.[19]

The U.S. side usually included participants as diverse as university department chairmen and high school Russian teachers. The Soviet
side seemed more uniform in that the participants were mostly *vuz* teachers. However, they represented a wide variety of institutions ranging
from strictly foreign language schools to technical schools of various
kinds. The 1977 exchange included teachers from the following Soviet
vuzy:

Alma-Ata Institute of Power
  Engineering

East Siberian Technological
  Institute, Ulan-Ude

Central State Institute of
  Physical Culture

Bauman Higher Technical
  School, Moscow

Moscow Institute of Physical
  Engineering

Moscow State University

Kemerovo State University

Gor'kiy Polytechnic Institute

Donetsk State University

Kazan' Civil Engineering
  Institute

Yerevan State University

Moscow Aviation Institute

Gor'kiy Pedagogical Institute
  of Foreign Languages

Dnepropetrovsk State University

M. Thorez State Pedagogical Institute of Foreign Languages, Moscow

Krasnodar Polytechnic Institute

Moscow Automobile and Road Construction Institute

Vilnius State University

Siberian Institute of Metallurgy (S. Ordzhonikidze), Novokuznetsk

Moscow Institute of Physical Engineering

Dnepropetrovsk Institute of Metallurgy

Moscow Institute of Steel and Alloys

N. Krupskaya Pedagogical Institute, Moscow

Kuybyshev Aviation Institute

Irkutsk Institute of Agriculture

Minsk State Pedagogical Institute of Foreign Languages

Leningrad State University

Tbilisi State University

V. Kuybyshev Finance and Economics Institute, Kazan'

Instruction for the Soviet teachers revolved around English as a foreign language, with emphasis on improving language skills, rather than on teaching methodology. Because the purpose of the program was to help the participants in the areas where they were weakest, they were assigned to smaller groups, each focusing on some difficult aspect of the English language. Americans studying Russian at MGU were given the same kind of instruction.

The program also stressed developing awareness of the respective cultures. For example, the Soviets traveled to several U.S. cities and visited art galleries, theaters, and other places of interest. Furthermore, they were given an allowance to buy their own books, food, and other necessities. In this way, they got a chance to fend for themselves in the American environment.[20]

The Soviets also engage in several other types of educational exchanges. These include work by biology, chemistry, mathematics, physics, and Russian-language teachers in developing countries and annual education exhibits in places as diverse as Chile, India, the United States, and West Germany.[21]

Such exchanges are administered by an office expressly devoted to that purpose in the Ministry of Education. According to Rosen, inspectors in that office are not fluent in foreign languages, but are education experts. They decide what teachers will go where, and for how long--months or years. In addition to sending teams abroad, the exchange office also organizes education exhibits and coordinates the preparation of publications on Soviet education for international organizations.[22]

Soviet multilateral contacts have taken place in international organizations like the United Nations Educational, Scientific and Cultural Organization (UNESCO). Since joining UNESCO in 1954, the Soviets have contributed to numerous UNESCO publications and participated in many UNESCO projects, especially those concerned with the eradication of illiteracy. They also provide scholarships to Third World students for study in the USSR under UNESCO auspices. Finally, the Soviets supply consultants and equipment for establishing educational institutions under UNESCO support in developing countries.[23]

Rosen notes that the USSR holds membership in a number of special UN agencies, some of whose activities relate to international education. For example, in 1956 the USSR ratified the minimum ages for industrial and nonindustrial employment of children set by the International Labor Organization.[24]

This section has discussed some of the special concerns and opportunities affecting professional Soviet educators in the foreign affairs field. Our examination of job placement indicated that the enthusiasm of young language teachers for jobs in rural areas may be low, that family influence can make a difference in whether or not a young person remains in the city, and that researchers can find assistant professorships at provincial universities without completing their graduate studies. If they are not Moscow-born, however, and want to remain in Moscow, they probably will need the support of a mentor powerful enough to find them permanent work in the capital. In addition, they will have to finish and defend their dissertation.

Although the Academy of Sciences institutes lead some fields of foreign area studies, they are not the only sources of expertise on the subject in the USSR. Apparently, other institutions—MGU, for example—can carve out areas of expertise that complement research taking place in the Academy institutes. The institutes may, however, enjoy an advantage in attracting talent because they are both teaching organizations and important research centers.

Bilateral and multilateral exchange agreements create special opportunities for Soviet teachers. In the foreign affairs field, language teachers probably benefit most from the exchanges, since they need not be as concerned with ideology as history and geography teachers. In fields such as mathematics and chemistry, teachers can work abroad in the developing countries, some staying months or even years. Finally, multilateral education projects such as those sponsored by UNESCO provide Soviet educators with the chance to interact with their counterparts around the world.

RESEARCH ORGANIZATIONS

Research Institutes under the Academy of Sciences

Considering the prominence of foreign language teaching in Soviet schools, the field of education represents the numerically largest source of employment for those trained in foreign languages and foreign area studies. As in American schools, teachers in Soviet primary and secondary schools do not normally devote time to research. Even the faculty members of Soviet *vuzy* concern themselves primarily with the training of the nation's future experts, not with systematic research. Moreover, university research tends to exhibit a strong academic orientation.

To deal with a spectrum of key issues--from foreign and security policy to economic, social, technological, and scientific matters--the Soviet government and party require an other than purely academic pool of foreign area specialists. These specialists must be professionally well trained, attuned to the needs of the policymaker, readily available for short-term consultation as well as for research in depth, and capable of providing scholarly justification for the Soviet regime's policies.

Much foreign area research is conducted in-house, by country desks and regional offices in government agencies, the CPSU Central Committee departments, the intelligence services, and the military establishment.

The government and party may also turn to specialized research institutions for in-depth information on the outside world.

The specialized research institutes are neither integral parts of the Soviet educational system nor components of the government, properly speaking, although they are under the control of the Council of Ministers. Although some have a long and respected scholarly tradition, most were established or reorganized in their present form in the 1960s and 1970s in response to the growing Soviet involvement with virtually every country of the world--communist and capitalist, developed and developing.

The majority of these policy-oriented institutes engaged in scholarly research are found under the umbrella of the prestigious USSR Academy of Sciences, an institution tracing its origins back to the early part of the 18th century.

The prominent scientists who are Academy members represent the major fields of scientific and scholarly inquiry conducted in the Academy's several hundred affiliated research institutes. Most of the institutes are concerned with the natural sciences and nationally important aspects of technology.[25] Three of the Academy's four operational divisions are therefore devoted to the natural sciences, while the fourth is concerned with research in the social sciences, including the humanities.

The foreign area research institutes are under the aegis of the Academy's Social Science Division, which is subdivided into the departments of History, Philosophy and Law, Economics, and Literature and Language. These traditional Soviet labels, however, no longer adequately describe the departments' research. Each department is responsible for a cluster of institutes assigned more or less well-defined tasks.

The 19 social science research institutes listed below both engage in foreign area research and provide postgraduate training in their specialty. They are the largest and most influential in information gathering and in policy analysis, planning, and implementation. All are located in Moscow.

The list, based on published Soviet and western sources and on interviews, divides the institutes into two categories: those engaged exclusively or primarily in foreign research and those with important foreign research interests. The assignment of institutes to the first category is based on information believed to be reliable. Assignments to the second category are more tentative.

Institutes of the USSR Academy of Sciences Engaged Primarily in Foreign Research

	Estimated Size of Specialist Staff
Institute of World Economy and International Relations (IMEMO)	600+
Institute of the International Workers Movement	?
Institute of World Literature	?
Institute of Linguistics	?
Institute of Africa (IA)	400+
Institute of the Far East (IDV)	?
Institute of Oriental Studies (IVAN)	600-850
Institute of Latin America (ILA)	?
Institute of the USA and Canada (IUSAC)	300+

Institutes of the USSR Academy of Sciences with Important Foreign Research Interests

Institute of World History

Institute of Ethnography

Institute of Linguistics

Institute of Slavic and Balkan Studies

Institute of the Economy of the World Socialist System

Institute of Economics

Institute of Systems Analysis

Institute of Scientific Information for the Social Sciences

Institute of Military History (jointly with Ministry of Defense)

Institute of History of Natural Sciences and Technology (?)

A complete listing of Academy of Sciences research facilities concerned with foreign countries would have to include those in the physical sciences and those outside Moscow. Several of those listed above have branches outside Moscow. In addition, several dozen less important research institutes attached to the academies of sciences of the various Soviet republics also engage in foreign research.

The Academy research institutes fall into two groups: the area-specific institutes engaged in research on a particular country or world region and those reflecting a functional approach and dealing across national boundaries with key economic or political problems. Best-known in the first category is IUSAC. Representative of the second category is the equally renowned IMEMO.

The research staff of most foreign area institutes is sufficiently large and diversified and so is the range of their research activity that each institute has several subsections. These interact to allow for interdisciplinary research on institute projects.

In 1979, the Academy leadership was composed of 753 members, including about one-third academicians (full members) and two-thirds corresponding members.[26] In terms of prestige and perquisites, they are at or near the pinnacle of the Soviet establishment. The vast majority of these eminent men are natural scientists. The total Academy research staff currently exceeds 46,000.[27] Basing our estimate on admittedly fragmentary information, we put the total of Academy-affiliated researchers primarily concerned with foreign area research at about 4000.

Researchers specializing in the study of foreign countries and international relations are called *mezhdunarodniki* (internationalists).[28] The degree of their influence is a subject of considerable controversy.[29] It is clear, however, that their upper echelons are consulted by party and government officials. They also have the important function of providing scholarly argumentation for Soviet policy perspectives and actions. A closer look at the activities and role of the institutes suggests that their utility to the regime varies substantially with the individual, his place in the institute hierarchy, and the nature of the institute itself.

In the earlier days of the Soviet regime, the upper level of the institute hierarchies tended to be composed of either older academics

or men with little substantive knowledge but strong ties to the party
leadership. Today, a new generation of institute directors is taking
over. They are generally well educated, but less academically oriented despite their doctoral degrees and high positions in the Academy
hierarchy.

The new institute directors are highly sensitive to the interests
of the Soviet regime and its leading figures and personally acquainted
with the power elite in government and party, in which they may have
served earlier in their careers. Some institute directors may be privy
to Soviet policymaking at the highest party levels through their high-
level contacts, and they may participate in it.

Georgiy Arbatov, who holds a doctoral degree in history and heads
the IUSAC, is both an academician and a full member of the CPSU Central
Committee. He apparently manages significant research tasks and information channels for the Soviet leadership.

Presumably waiting on the lower rungs of the ladder leading to influence within the Soviet elite establishment are the younger institute
directors like Dr. Evgeniy Primakov and Dr. Anatoliy Gromyko. Primakov
directs the large Institute of Oriental Studies; he had formerly been
a deputy director of IMEMO. Prior to that, he had served from 1962 to
1970 on the Asian and African desk of *Pravda*.

Gromyko, son of the Soviet foreign minister and Politburo member,
heads the Academy's Institute of Africa, which has gained in importance
with the growing Soviet role in that part of the world.[30] Neither of
the two men fits the mold of the old-time institute scholar. They show
a lively interest in the contemporary foreign scene, appear regularly
on the foreign propaganda broadcasts of Radio Moscow, and participate
frequently in other Soviet media activities.

We have only limited information on the second echelon staff members of the Academy institutes--those who serve as the principal analysts or direct the junior staffs. What we know points to a background
in elite higher education and often to prior experience in government
agencies or party offices. Conspicuous among them because of their
rank and impressive background are several retired high-ranking military officers, including Generals V. Larionov, N. Lomov, and M.
Mil'shteyn, associated with institute work on defense and arms control.

Reportedly, government and party officials attend one or another Academy institute part time as candidates for advanced academic degrees (and career advancement). Soviet foreign ministry officials are particularly well represented in that regard because of the coincidence of their staff members' educational background and professional interests.[31]

In early 1980, Boris N. Ponomarev, candidate Politburo member in charge of the Central Committee's International Department, presented the Institute of Oriental Studies with the Order of the Red Banner of Labor.[32] In Soviet practice this honor could signify only that the party leadership was satisfied with the work of the institute and its director, Academician Primakov.

The Soviet leadership apparently is also satisfied with the work of the other social science institutes of the Academy of Sciences. Neither Brezhnev's speech at the 26th CPSU Congress in 1981 nor the guidelines for future development that the congress adopted criticized the Academy's social science work. This has not always been the case.

Earlier party congresses frequently took the institutes to task for being insufficiently effective in serving Soviet interests. Criticism was invariably followed by organizational shake-ups of the targeted institutes or at least by the replacement of their directors. At times, such criticisms have foreshadowed the establishment of new institutes aimed at filling gaps in the Academy's social science research structure.

The Academy of Sciences is now apparently meeting the demands of the regime insofar as the production of information and analyses of the contemporary foreign scene is concerned. Relations between the institutes and the party and government seem to have entered an era of stability.[33]

Three major trends in the Academy's foreign area research have become apparent in the past decade. They have implications for the type of professional personnel required by present conditions and for the employment trend for such personnel.

In the first place, the pressure of government and party requirements has forcibly redirected Soviet foreign area research from its

traditional linguistic and ethnographic focus to a concern with the
contemporary world and its problems (although traditional studies continue to be produced in the universities and in institutes of both the
USSR Academy and its republic counterparts). Presumably the new focus
will mean a continued expansion of Soviet foreign area research staffs
throughout the government, party, education, and academia. It will
also mean the growing predominance on such staffs of scholar-analysts
able to work in the academic community, government agencies, party
committees, and the media.

Second, the growing Soviet political, economic, and military role
worldwide has sharply increased the demand for specialists on hitherto
neglected geographic areas. Some idea of the tremendous growth of Soviet foreign area research can be gained from the case of African studies conducted under the auspices of the USSR Academy.

During the 1970s, a number of research institutes turned their
attention to African political, economic, social and cultural developments. At present, the following institutes of the Academy of Sciences,
in addition to the Institute of Africa, are conducting research on
Africa: Oriental Studies, Ethnography, Economics, World Economy and
International Relations, Economics of the World Socialist System,
Geography, State and Law, Linguistics, Philosophy, International Workers Movement, World Literature, and World History.[34] This example also
illustrates the difficulty of assessing quantitatively the present
status of the vast and diversified Soviet effort to develop an adequate
foreign area research capability.

The third trend stems from the Soviet goal of overtaking the United
States and the western industrialized nations. Quite apart from an increasing attention to the political, economic and military policies and
conditions in those countries, Soviet specialists are now systematically
studying western, especially American, organizational, administrative,
and methodological concepts and innovational techniques.

The creation in 1976 within the Academy system of an Institute of
Systems Research, headed by Dr. Dzhermen Gvishiani, academician and
deputy chairman of the State Committee for Science and Technology

(GKNT) symbolizes this trend. The trend will further encourage the demand for double area specialists, that is, individuals combining administrative, managerial, technical, and other professional expertise with
foreign area training.[35]

Other Research Organizations

Other organizations in addition to the Academy of Sciences institutes engage in foreign affairs research in the USSR. Some are attached
to functional entities in the government and so can be thought of as emphasizing research directly applicable to government missions. Others
are oriented toward academia and probably away from applied research.[36]

The Research Institute of Economic and Technical Cooperation. The
State Committee for Economic Relations with Foreign Countries manages
Soviet foreign aid programs in the Third World--a mission that has
proved increasingly complicated over the past 20 years as Soviet activities in the Third World have increased.[37] Apparently because of this
expanded mission, the Research Institute of Economic and Technical Cooperation was established within GKES in January 1979.

The USSR's foreign aid clients have complained repeatedly about de-
lays in construction, unanticipated local costs, and Moscow's failure
to provide turnkey projects. To remedy these problems, the 120 staff
members of the institute are examining ways to improve (1) the implementation of aid projects and (2) the marketing and after-sales service
of Soviet machinery and equipment provided under economic aid
agreements. They are also searching for new aid opportunities, particularly in energy and metallurgy, and for better ways to evaluate the
progress of aid programs.[38]

The Research Institute of Economic and Technical Cooperation is
clearly a problem-solving organization. It was formed to help GKES fulfill its mission, and seems to have visibility and staff enough to
succeed.

The Scientific Research Marketing Institute. Another interesting
example of a government organization carrying out foreign area research
is the Ministry of Foreign Trade's Scientific Research Marketing Institute (NIKI). According to Blair Ruble, "the institute conducts research

of a purely applied nature."[39]   Its job is to find profitable markets
abroad for Soviet products. It also conducts research in market fore-
casting and techniques of international trade.

NIKI's staff of over 350 work in six sections: Foreign Economic
Systems, Commodity Markets, Prices, Foreign Commercial Information,
Statistics, and Foreign Companies. The institute's main facilities
are located in Moscow, and it also has a branch in Leningrad. NIKI researchers work closely with trade officials throughout Eastern Europe
and conduct joint research with Eastern European trade ministries.
NIKI publishes a *Bulletin of Foreign Commercial Information* and numerous reports on market opportunities worldwide.[40]

Thus, NIKI answers a wide spectrum of requirements generated by
the Soviet Foreign Trade Ministry. The institute is not only a source
of data, it is also a source of analysis and practical proposals about
how to improve the USSR's foreign trade.

University and Republic Academy of Sciences Research Centers. Outside of the ministry system, foreign affairs research centers are part
of universities and the republic academies of sciences. These organizations seem to concentrate on theoretical work, leaving applied research to the ministry institutes and the USSR Academy of Sciences institutes.

There are perhaps a few exceptions to this rule, including Moscow
State University's Laboratory for the Study of the USA, Leningrad State
University's Oriental Faculty, and the Group for the Study of Economic
Problems of African Nations at Kiev State University. Each of these
three centers apparently maintains close contact with institutes conducting related research, particularly in the USSR Academy of Sciences.
To the extent that Soviet policymakers directly task such networks for
information upon which to base decisions, the institutes involved can
be considered to conduct applied research.[41]

Applied research is also conducted in linguistics in republic institutes. A strong center for applied linguistics grew up in Tashkent
in the 1920s as part of efforts to develop written alphabets for Central Asian languages.[42]   The process of writing down and characterizing
national languages, which apparently continues today, contributes to

better language teaching methods. Perhaps Soviet military and civilian advisers are currently applying these efforts in Afghanistan.

To return to our earlier point, however, most research done in universities and republic academies of sciences appears to be theoretical. Many of the institutes, especially in the Caucasus, Central Asia, and the Far East, are devoted to oriental studies. These programs frequently focus on a nationality's language, history, and culture; philology is the commonest focus of research. Table 9 gives an idea of the variety of oriental studies programs in existence in the USSR.

Table 9

FOREIGN AFFAIRS RESEARCH ORGANIZATIONS AFFILIATED
WITH REPUBLIC ACADEMIES AND UNIVERSITIES[43]

Institutes and Sponsoring Organizations	Specialties
Institute of the Peoples of the Near and Middle East, Azerbaydzhan Academy of Sciences, Baku	Turkic, Iranian, Arabic philology
Institute of Oriental Studies, Armenian Academy of Sciences, Yerevan	Byzantine, Iranian, Arabic studies; emphasis on philology
Institute of Oriental Studies, Georgian Academy of Sciences, Tbilisi	Byzantine, Iranian, Semitic studies
Institute of Oriental Studies, Tadzhik Academy of Sciences, Dushanbe	Turkic, Iranian philology
Institute of Oriental Studies, Uzbek Academy of Sciences, Tashkent	Turkic, Iranian, Arabic, Sinic studies
Faculty of Oriental Studies, Azerbaydzhan State University, Baku	Arabic, Persian, Turkic philology
Faculty of Oriental Studies, Tbilisi State University, Tbilisi	Iranian, Turkic, Semitic philology
Faculty of Oriental Languages, Tadzhik State University, Dushanbe	Arabic, Iranian philology
Oriental Faculty, Tashkent State University, Tashkent	Turkic, Iranian, Arabic philology
Department of General Turkic and Dungan[a] Studies, Kirgiz Academy of Sciences, Frunze	Dungan studies
Oriental Faculty, Far Eastern State University, Vladivostok	Chinese, Japanese philology

[a]Tribe of Mongolized Turks in Turkestan.

Oriental studies have an important place in the history of Russian and Soviet foreign area scholarship. St. Petersburg (now Leningrad) was an internationally known oriental studies center at the end of the 19th century, and several Central Asian and Far Eastern research centers—notably Tashkent and Vladivostok—were established before 1930.[44]

We find it interesting, however, that other foreign area specialties—American, European, and African studies—have found a limited place in Soviet research organizations outside Moscow, Leningrad, and Kiev. It seems that the Caucasian, Central Asian, and Far Eastern research institutes were deemed suitable for oriental studies, but not for other foreign area specialties. In short, if a scholar wants to pursue serious research on the United States or Europe, he probably must go to Moscow.[45]

Looking beyond the USSR Academy of Sciences institutes, we see two basic types of research organizations in the foreign affairs field. The first type is sponsored by government agencies and answers to the missions of those agencies through applied research projects. The second type is attached to universities or republic academies of sciences and usually engages in theoretical research. Exceptions to this rule seem to occur when a research organization maintains close ties with an institute of the USSR Academy of Sciences or emphasizes applied linguistics.

Aside from oriental studies, limited opportunities for foreign affairs research appear to exist outside Moscow, Leningrad, and Kiev. This tendency, however, seems consonant with the Soviet penchant for regional divisions of labor, whether in economic development, industrial production, or intellectual activity. Hence, the Soviets would probably accept as natural an emphasis on Turkic and Iranian studies in Central Asia and on Japanese and Chinese studies in the Far East. Only Moscow seems to combine all foreign area specialties in one urban center.

THE MEDIA

In recent years, the international facets of Soviet information and communication activities have developed at a rate reflecting the

increasing geographic scope and importance of Soviet global involvement.
We found this to be true of every major manifestation of information
and communication employing international specialists: foreign news
coverage and analysis of international developments; worldwide information-gathering efforts; publication of journals, pamphlets, popular
books, and specialized studies concerned with foreign nations; distribution of these publications, in both Russian and foreign languages
at home and abroad; translation programs focused on foreign technical
and scientific literature, but not limited to it; and broadcasts in the
world's major and many of its minor languages and dialects, beamed regularly to every continent.

The magnitude of this massive Soviet information, analytic, and
propaganda effort points to an organizational apparatus worthy of a
superpower. While comparisons between the USSR and United States in
this as in other regards are hazardous, we nevertheless suggest that the
United States appears to be falling behind in the area of international
communication, especially where the use of foreign languages by media
personnel is concerned.

The Soviet media today can draw on the talents of a vast and diversified corps of full-time foreign area specialists, linguists, translators, and staffs combining professional training with linguistic and
country expertise. They are assisted by prestigious foreign area specialists drawn from the ranks of the area institutes of the USSR Academy
of Sciences and of party officials concerned with coordination of Soviet
activities and policies in the international arena. Such experts can
speak with authority in the columns of *Pravda* or expound the Soviet view
of world events in Arabic and other foreign language broadcasts.[46]

Journalism can be rewarding for the Soviet specialist embarking on
a career in international affairs. His educational background and professional qualifications tend to be similar to those of a junior diplomat. A successful career in journalism may bring him to the attention
of the government and party elite and open the way to key assignments.

Leonid Zamyatin is a good example. Zamyatin rose through the
ranks of the TASS news agency to become its general director. In 1978,
he went from there to the influential and politically sensitive position

of chief of the Central Committee's information department, serving in
this capacity as a principal spokesman for the Soviet leadership.
Other outstanding media figures co-opted by the foreign ministry have
attained ambassadorial rank.[47]

The perquisites associated with international journalism--espe-
cially travel abroad and a more exciting life-style than that of the
ordinary Soviet bureaucrat--also draw gifted (or well-connected) young
people into careers in the media. This may be one reason why so many
children and relatives of the Soviet leadership are to be found in the
communication field.[48]

Pravda, the CPSU organ, and *Izvestiya*, the voice of the Soviet
government, with a combined circulation in 1976 of 18.6 million,[49] are
the two most authoritative newspapers in all matters of Soviet policy.
Although both make use of news agency reports, they maintain their own
sizable staff of foreign correspondents in the major world capitals and
employ an array of international specialists in their Moscow home
offices.

TASS and Novosti, the two principal Soviet news agencies, also
make considerable use of personnel trained in foreign affairs and languages. TASS, under the Council of Ministers, functions as the official Soviet press agency; Novosti, controlled by a group of cultural,
information, and propaganda organizations, is ostensibly unofficial.
Both are in fact closely supervised by the Soviet government and party
apparatus and operate as their instruments.

The missions of TASS and Novosti go beyond the collection and
distribution of news. These organizations also make the preliminary
political and propagandistic evaluation of the information they gather
for eventual dissemination at home and abroad. This policy function
requires a close working relationship between the news agencies and
the major elements of the Soviet power structure.

Hence, the foreign affairs staff of TASS and Novosti must possess
both international expertise and a high degree of sensitivity to shifting Soviet policy requirements. This may be another reason why these
news agencies are often viewed as way stations to important government
and party positions concerned with international affairs.

TASS reportedly supplies some 4000 Soviet newspapers with news.[50]
It also provides Radio Moscow with the bulk of its material. The information thus disseminated originates with TASS correspondents operating out of the approximately 100 bureaus that the agency currently
maintains abroad.[51] According to Sergey Losev, general director of
TASS, these correspondents must know two foreign languages and have
"an excellent knowledge of the history, politics, economics, culture
and customs of the peoples of the country or region of residence."[52]

At TASS headquarters in Moscow, staff members are normally assigned to either the foreign or domestic news division. The international affairs division, said to employ the agency's elite personnel,[53]
is subdivided into geographic desks maintaining direct daily contact
with TASS correspondents abroad.

The international affairs division of TASS employs its own translating staff capable of handling the large quantities of materials selected from foreign newspapers that reach the agency's editorial offices
from all over the world. Some of these translations are used in the
preparation of Soviet news releases or foreign policy commentaries. A
select portion of this documentation, together with items not so widely
circulated, is transmitted daily to key Soviet officials for background
information in formulating policy.

TASS also handles the equally important flow of information from
the USSR to the outside world. The TASS editorial staff packages news
items regarding Soviet developments, policies, and perspectives on international issues for free distribution to some 350 foreign press
agencies in about 80 countries. Such information is supplied where
suitable in the Russian language (presumably that is the case in Eastern
Europe) or where more appropriate in one of the major foreign languages,
including English, German, Spanish, and Arabic. The selection of suitable items for a foreign audience necessarily requires a staff attuned
to the needs of the potential foreign client.

The translation of TASS materials into foreign languages for dissemination abroad in turn increases the need for linguistic talent on
the staff of TASS. The impressive dimensions of these various international TASS activities, and by implication the size of the agency's

international specialist staff, can be gauged by its large annual budget, reportedly amounting at present to the equivalent of $550 mil-
lion.[54] Both TASS and Novosti have exchange-of-information agreements
with numerous foreign press services and other interested parties.[55]

The international activities of Novosti are even more far-flung
than those of TASS. The Novosti press agency was established in 1961
to promote cultural relations with foreign countries and to serve Soviet political ends more flexibly than the official news service, TASS,
is in a position to do. The official founder of Novosti was the Union
of Soviet Societies for Friendship and Cultural Relations with Foreign
Countries, whose foreign associates--constituting ready-made channels
for Novosti news releases and publications--are now reportedly found in
126 countries.[56]

Novosti maintains its own correspondents in some 80 countries and
distributes news releases and feature articles on Soviet life to the
foreign press and to publishing houses in 110 countries.[57] It claims
to conduct information exchanges with more than 7000 foreign newspapers
and magazines and with 120 foreign publishing firms, transmitting in
the process some 60,000 articles a year.[58]

The Novosti news agency doubles as a major publishing house for
foreign language books and pamphlets intended for distribution abroad.
Reportedly, this literature is published in 50 languages with a combined printing exceeding 15 million copies a year.[59] In addition,
Novosti prepares some 50 periodicals in various languages and dialects.

The scope of Novosti's foreign-language activity can be illus-
trated by the case of India. The USSR has for two decades sought to
promote a favorable atmosphere there for Soviet-Indian cooperation. In
support of this objective, Novosti publishes a magazine, *Soviet Land*,
in 12 Indian languages. Another Novosti-sponsored publication, *Sputnik*,
has a wider geographic distribution. *Sputnik*, a general interest
monthly, appears in English, French, German, and Urdu.

Some Soviet foreign-language publications address themselves to
special groups, such as youth or women. *Soviet Woman* is among the better
known. It is printed, in addition to Russian, in English, French, German, Spanish, Hungarian, Chinese, Hindi, Bengali, Japanese, Korean, and

Arabic. The well-known weekly *Moscow News* was initially meant for the foreigner traveling in the USSR, but its English, Spanish, French, and Arabic editions are now being distributed worldwide.

The trend appears to be toward the publication of an increasing number of foreign-language versions of major periodicals read by the Soviet professionals. *International Affairs* (published in two foreign languages), *Foreign Trade* (four languages), and *Far Eastern Affairs* (three foreign languages) fit into this steadily growing category; *New Times* (ten foreign languages) may perhaps also be included. The Academy of Sciences recently announced that it will publish a new periodical, *Science in the USSR*, in Russian and English.

Russian is not widely understood outside the USSR (with the possible exception of the Slavic portions of Eastern Europe),[60] but it is also not understood to a surprising extent inside the USSR. The millions of Soviet citizens belonging to non-Russian ethnic groups often possess only a limited knowledge of the Russian language. Translation is therefore a major professional activity inside the USSR, providing steady employment for thousands of foreign-language specialists.

The Center for the Translation of Scientific and Technical Literature and Documentation in Moscow, and several other Soviet translation agencies, systematically and in considerable detail examine western technological literature. They index, translate, and abstract much of it for circulation among interested parties. In 1979 alone, close to 2000 foreign titles were translated from some 100 foreign languages, about 75 percent into Russian and the rest into other Soviet languages, for a total output of 113 million printed copies.[61]

Three languages of the industrialized West--English, German, and French--predominate among those from which the Soviet government selects items to be translated. In large part this emphasis reflects the technological and scientific leadership of the countries in which these languages are spoken. The importance of English as a channel to the outside world is reflected in the fact that one-third of all titles translated from foreign languages into Russian or other Soviet languages are translated from English. German and French play a lesser role, accounting for 330 and 169 titles, respectively, of the 1945 titles translated.

Another major employer of international affairs specialists and
commentators, foreign area experts, and linguists is the international
radio broadcasting service of the USSR. Its stations include Radio
Moscow and Radio Peace and Progress. Other regional and special (including clandestine) stations have a more limited mission and reach.

The Soviet international broadcast system, under the direction of
the State Commission for Television and Radio Broadcasting, has grown
into a major operation now broadcasting over 2000 hours per week to
virtually every country in the world. English-language broadcasts,
like English-language publications, are particularly emphasized (there
is now a 24-hour English-language service), but the Third World is by
no means neglected. In 1980 the Soviets were broadcasting in 11 African languages (as against three for the BBC).[62] For obvious reasons,
Afghanistan constitutes a special target, at present receiving broadcasts in Dari as well as Pashto.

Soviet international radio currently beams 63 foreign languages
abroad. We were able to determine neither the size of the staff engaged in these global broadcast activities nor the extent to which the
operations make use of foreign personnel (drawn primarily, we assume,
from the more than 50,000 foreign students now at Soviet educational
institutions). A comparison with the personnel requirements of the
Voice of America might provide a basis for at least a rough estimate.

GOVERNMENT AGENCIES

Almost every national-level ministry, state committee, and other
agency in the USSR contains some kind of international office. The
Ministry of the Electrical Equipment Industry has a Main Administration
for Electrical Machines Abroad, as well as a Foreign Relations Department. The Ministry of the Gas Industry has both a Foreign Relations
Administration and an All-Union Association (*vsesoyuznoye ob"yedineniye*)
for the Construction of Gas Industry Enterprises Abroad. An *association*
in this context is roughly equivalent to a firm in the United States;
the term *all-union* indicates that the association is at the national
(rather than republic or local) level. The State Committee for Science
and Technology administers several internationally oriented offices,

including the Administration for Scientific-Technical Cooperation with
Capitalist and Developing Countries and an all-union association,
Vneshtekhnika, which is active in scientific and technical exchange
with foreign countries.[63]

Of necessity, this report examines only a limited number of organizations employing foreign area specialists. To cover both agencies
that deal with foreign countries more or less on a full-time basis and
those whose main mission is in another area, but whose foreign contacts
may be an important aspect of their activities, we discuss the production ministries in general terms and the Ministry of Foreign Affairs
and the State Committee for Science and Technology in some detail.

The Ministry of Foreign Affairs

The Soviet Ministry of Foreign Affairs is "a mirror of Western
Foreign Offices."[64] Like the U.S. Department of State, it is divided
along geographic and functional lines. The organization of the geographic departments indicates the importance or accessibility to the
Soviets of different areas of the world. Three departments--one each
for North Africa, sub-Saharan coastal states, and East and South
Africa--cover Africa, while Latin America is handled by only one. Six
departments deal with Europe. The Near and Middle East each rates a
department, as does the United States.[65]

In addition to the 17 geographic departments, there are 9 function-
al departments and numerous bureaus and administrations. The functional
offices include consular, protocol, treaty and legal, and translation.
Important research and analysis groups include the Administration for
Foreign Policy Planning and the Administration for General International
Problems.

The Soviet foreign ministry has at least one functional office
whose responsibilities are usually not taken up by foreign ministries
in the West: the Administration for Servicing the Diplomatic Corps
(UpDK). UpDK assigns living quarters and a maid to foreign diplomats,
gets theater tickets for them, finds places for their children in Soviet schools, issues them driver's licenses, and even grants them access
to fishing and hunting preserves.[66]

UpDK also provides chauffeurs, maids, cooks and secretaries to western commercial firms with offices in Moscow. UpDK secretaries may be quite competent and they may be given considerable responsibility. For example, if a western firm has only one Moscow representative who travels frequently, his UpDK secretary in effect maintains the firm's Moscow operations for long periods of time in his absence.

A second functional department without precise counterpart in western foreign ministries is the Tenth Department, responsible for ensuring the security of Soviet embassy operations abroad. Although organizationally subordinate to the Ministry of Foreign Affairs, the Tenth Department is apparently managed directly by the KGB.[67] In effect, it is a counterintelligence office within the Soviet foreign ministry.

A young foreign affairs specialist is accepted into the diplomatic corps with the rank of *stazher* (probationer). If successful, he may then move up through the ranks to attache, third secretary, second secretary, first secretary, counselor, minister, and ambassador.[68] Emigre accounts suggest that the diplomatic corps has stringent entrance requirements stemming from security considerations related to the diplomat's need to live and travel abroad. According to Kaznacheev, an aspiring diplomat must be deemed loyal, trustworthy, and able before he will be considered for a lifelong career in the foreign service.[69]

The State Committee for Science and Technology (GKNT)

The State Committee of the USSR Council of Ministers for Science and Technology was formed in 1965 to serve as a conduit for high-level Soviet leadership decisions about progress and priorities in scientific research and development. That is, it was designed as a science policy agency that sets goals for Soviet R&D and tries to see that they are carried out.

Officially, only one of the five major functions through which the committee performs this mission is devoted to foreign affairs. This function involves arranging foreign contacts for Soviet researchers.[70]

Unofficially, GKNT's most important function is to manage the acquisition of foreign technology, whether through covert or overt means. The committee serves as a point of central control, drawing up priorities on what technologies should be sought, and how. GKNT bases these judgments on the comprehensive investigation of foreign technology sources conducted by its staff members.[71]

GKNT's international work is handled by several offices. The Administration for Scientific-Technical Cooperation with Capitalist and Developing Countries investigates foreign technology sources and negotiates cooperation agreements between western firms and GKNT.[72] A similar administration handles this function for the socialist countries. Divided into geographic sections, these administrations perform such tasks as selecting representatives for bilateral commissions, making conference and travel arrangements, and providing escort service for foreign visitors.

The other international agency in GKNT, *Vneshtekhnika*, negotiates contracts involving technical cooperation. According to Louvan Nolting, *Vneshtekhnika* arranges initial contracts to conduct joint research, cooperate in prototype manufacture, exchange data, or arrange site visits for technical experts.[73]

The committee's all-embracing control over scientific and technical cooperation does not officially include commercial transactions. Once GKNT decides to acquire a particular technology from a foreign country, the related activities are considered commercial and fall under the jurisdiction of the Ministry of Foreign Trade (MFT) and the appropriate foreign trade organizaions.[74]

GKNT's high-level mission, however, apparently places it in conflict with the MFT on many of these issues. For example, the ministry is supposed to consult with the committee on contracts involving technology. This requirement means that the ministry may be subject to the committee's review for any but the most straightforward commodity purchases.[75]

The staffs of the GKNT international offices tend to be foreign area specialists rather than scientists. Many seem to come from the Academy of Sciences institutes with advanced degrees and excellent foreign language skills. Personnel working on U.S. exchanges may have been trained at IUSAC, spent time in the United States, and transferred to GKNT from another job in *amerikanistika*.

Having less than 200 professionals, GKNT is a small bureaucracy by Soviet standards. It does not have the time to train new employees; once hired, a staff member must be prepared to take up a heavy load.[76] He may immediately be thrust into, say, answering correspondence from western scientists wondering whether their Soviet counterparts would deliver draft papers in time for a conference, prodding the Soviet counterparts to complete the drafts, and then helping to review the drafts before sending them abroad.

GKNT's most important work requires a comprehensive, up-to-date grasp of scientific and technological development abroad. Thus, the committee also provides substantial employment opportunities for double area specialists who combine technical expertise with knowledge of lan- guages and advanced western societies. These specialists follow for- eign accomplishments in science and technology through a systematic study of foreign literature, either in the original or in translation.

Foreign area and double area specialists in the State Committee for Science and Technology probably are among the best available in the USSR. Many have advanced degrees from elite *vuzy* and are fluent in foreign languages. They seem able to perform effectively in a small bureaucracy where considerable responsibility is thrust upon them.

The Production Ministries

Most production ministries have their own in-house foreign area expertise.[77] Small ministries and branch offices of large ministries in small cities, however, must rely on Intourist, the government tour- ist agency, for help with foreign visitors.

Typically, midlevel staff members in ministry foreign relations departments are 25 to 35 years old, fluent in one or two languages, and expert in whatever technical area their ministry emphasizes. For example, an employee of the Foreign Relations Department of the Min- istry of the Electrical Equipment Industry may speak English and German and have a degree in electrical engineering.

Only rarely would a production ministry employee have sophistication in foreign area studies beyond languages and his ministry's business. He would not have studied international affairs and would have little knowledge of western politics, economics, and society. If he does have such knowledge, he probably began his career in the Ministry of Foreign Trade or has a second job with the KGB.

In short, officers in ministry foreign relations departments are not polished products of MGIMO and the Academy of Sciences institutes. They probably began their careers in the ministry structure, acquired languages along the way, and ended up employed in foreign affairs. Their foreign language skills are probably adequate and attuned to the vocabulary needed for their ministry's work. However, they may not speak the flawless English, German, French, or Japanese expected of an MGIMO graduate.

On the job, such staff members probably spend much of their time running errands, arranging the details of meetings, and shuttling foreign visitors around town. Unlike their counterparts at the Academy of Sciences, they apparently do not travel abroad, the ultimate perquisite in the Soviet system. They are expected to help foreign businessmen, but not, as members of the Soviet foreign affairs community, to influence them.

A western businessman trying to arrange a deal would not approach officials in the foreign relations department of a ministry for a decision; he would go higher up in the ministry structure. However, he might turn to the foreign relations staff for advice on the best time and method for approaching the higher-ups.

The farther a western businessman travels outside Moscow, the more likely he is to encounter incompetence in both language skills and technical knowledge. Two factors contribute to this difference: first, regional offices must sometimes depend on nontechnical translators from Intourist; second, provincial in-house technical translators have limited contacts with foreigners and thus get few opportunities to practice their skills.

Differences among the several types of foreign-area-related positions in the Soviet government involve the differences between foreign

area and double area specialties. A chauffeur employed by the foreign
ministry's UpDK must have some language training before going to work
for foreign diplomats. In that way, he can eavesdrop as well as drive.
An electrical engineer at the Ministry of the Electrical Equipment Industry must know at least one foreign language if he works in the ministry's Foreign Relations Department. A staff member in one of the
international offices of the State Committee for Science and Technology
may have more than language skills. He may be a true foreign area specialist, perhaps with a degree from a prestigious institution.

In sum, Soviet government agencies with international missions
need both foreign area and double area specialists. The Ministry of
Foreign Affairs hires foreign area specialists for diplomatic work and
double area personnel, ranging from cooks and maids to lawyers and
economists, to service foreign diplomats in the USSR. The State Committee for Science and Technology hires foreign area specialists to arrange foreign contacts for Soviet scientists and double area specialists to carry out its unofficial, but vitally important, function of
acquiring foreign technology.

PARTY ORGANIZATIONS

The Politburo of the CPSU Central Committee "is clearly the paramount collegial organ for the formulation of Soviet foreign policy."[78]
The Secretariat and departments of the CPSU Central Committee augment
or support the Politburo's work on foreign policy.

Members of the Central Committee Secretariat make many routine
decisions in foreign policy and in other areas. This *de facto* delegation of decisionmaking power from the Politburo to the Secretariat pre-
vents the Politburo from being seriously overburdened by detail.

The Central Committee departments provide the staff work on which
the Politburo and Secretariat base their decisions. This staffing requirement makes the Central Committee departments an important source
of employment for foreign area specialists.

Several Central Committee departments contribute to the making of
Soviet foreign policy, including Cadres Abroad, International, International Information, and Liaison with Communist and Workers' Parties

of Socialist Countries. Our discussion of the role that foreign area specialists play in party organizations will concentrate on the activities of the International Department.[79]

The International Department is headed by Boris Ponomarev, a powerful party executive who has long been associated with Soviet foreign policy. Ponomarev apparently is the premier official responsible for organizing party staff work in the international field.[80]

The focus of the International Department appears to have shifted during the Brezhnev era from relations with nonruling communist parties to intergovernmental relations.[81] Whereas before 1970 Ponomarev met publicly only with foreign communists and representatives of radical Third World regimes, since then he has met increasingly with leaders of the major western countries and Japan.[82]

The International Department's intergovernmental role both complements and conflicts with the diplomatic mission of the Ministry of Foreign Affairs. The department does not routinely take over the official duties of the foreign ministry, either in Moscow or in foreign capitals. However, as Leonard Shapiro points out, "the MFA has no political muscle whatever," while the International Department most definitely has.[83]

Thus, the International Department seems to work behind the scene, gathering information and making a case for a particular policy direction. Meanwhile, the foreign ministry carries on the routine work of international diplomacy--its recognized and important domain. However, because the International Department "is the element in the Soviet decision-making process which gathers information [and] briefs the Politburo," it strongly influences Soviet foreign policy.[84]

Since the mid-1960s, the International Department has been recruiting academic foreign area specialists such as those in the Academy of Sciences institutes.[85] All but one of Ponomarev's deputies graduated from prestigious institutions with degrees in area studies and international relations. All but one hold the degree of *doktor nauk*,[86] and all actively teach and publish in their fields. The International Department also has staff members with practical experience in journalism or the diplomatic service.[87]

On a different level, the International Department hires consultants from the universities and Academy of Sciences institutes. These consultants are evidently established scholars who either become full-time staff members or retain their positions elsewhere while working part time for the department. According to Ben Fischer, the consultants are probably "the main working channel which runs between the Department and the foreign policy think tanks organized under the USSR Academy of Sciences."[88]

At the entry level, International Department staff members may sometimes be recruited into the department while working for such organizations as the Committee for the Defense of Peace and the Committee for Solidarity with Asian and African Countries. These organizations are a major International Department responsibility because they serve as mechanisms for establishing links with radical or sympathetic groups abroad. They also serve as a natural recruiting ground for young talent.

For example, a typical entry-level staff member may have been attending graduate school at the same time that he was working for the peace or the solidarity committee. There he would have come into contact with the International Department personnel directing the committee. If the student showed political and academic talent, he may have been offered a job in the International Department.[89]

The International Department of the CPSU Central Committee seems to employ about 150 well-educated, highly qualified foreign area specialists in Moscow.[90] These people are not mere communist party bureaucrats, but trained specialists in foreign policy, public opinion, and economic, social, and political conditions in their major country areas. Their analyses, conclusions, and recommendations may become the foreign policy of the USSR, for they are closer to the top leadership than most in the Soviet foreign area specialist community.

MILITARY ORGANIZATIONS

We examine here two aspects of Soviet military activities in the foreign affairs field: first, research and the relationship between research and policymaking and, second, military missions abroad. Our discussion of research concentrates on the General Staff Academy and its foreign-area-related work; our discussion of military missions concentrates on the various duties of Soviet military personnel abroad.

The General Staff Academy

The General Staff Academy is the foremost military research institute involved in foreign area studies. The academy receives its research tasks directly from the Minister of Defense and the Chief of the General Staff and cooperates with other Ministry of Defense organizations on work involving, according to General of the Army V. G. Kulikov, "the most important problems of military science."[91] In the international field, these problems include post-World War II "local wars of imperialism" like Korea and Vietnam and the organization, armament, and military theories of the largest "capitalist" armies.[92]

Practically speaking, research work in these areas involves poring over the formidable mass of written material--periodical literature, books, and monographs--about western armed forces. Researchers at the General Staff Academy must therefore possess two types of foreign area expertise: language training and an understanding of western military science.[93]

Harriet and William F. Scott have noted that the General Staff Academy performs research that Pentagon study and analysis groups and contract research firms would perform in the United States.[94] Any such research organization is concerned about the usefulness of its products to high-level policymakers. The General Staff Academy is directly tasked by the highest military authorities--the Minister of Defense and Chief of the General Staff--so we may assume that its products are useful to them.

The General Staff Academy has probably contributed a considerable body of research on strategic arms limitation. According to Thomas W. Wolfe, both the Ministry of Defense and the General Staff have had active roles in the strategic arms limitation talks (SALT), although the General Staff has usually provided most of the military representation on the Soviet SALT delegation.[95] One or both almost certainly (1) provide the position papers underlying the military's perspective on SALT and (2) mediate the differences with regard to SALT among the various armed services.[96] Much of the background research needed for these tasks has probably been provided by the General Staff Academy.

Each of the Soviet armed services has its own staff of professional military personnel, many of whom are experts on their counterpart services in, say, NATO or China. These staff officers probably also have foreign language skills useful to them in their work.

Soviet Military Advisers Abroad

According to the Central Intelligence Agency, almost 16,000 Soviets and Eastern Europeans were serving as military advisers in the Third World in 1979. The USSR provided most of the supporting services needed for assembling equipment, training Third World personnel in the use and maintenance of equipment, and advising Third World commanders.[97]

Who are these military aid technicians? Are they actually officers and enlisted men in the Soviet armed forces, or are they civilians employed by Soviet defense industries? Are they trained in African, Asian, and Middle Eastern languages? Do they mix well with their Third World clients?

To most of these questions we have found no answers, except the suggestion that heavy-handed Soviet methods sometimes alienate local personnel.[98] We do not know, for example, whether the Soviet personnel must work with translators, live in isolated compounds, and otherwise follow rules that would limit their effectiveness as aid technicians.

A more serious military aid relationship has evolved in Afghanistan over the past three years. Even before Soviet combat troops invaded in December 1979, Soviet military advisers were taking over positions in the Afghan Ministry of Defense and in the upper echelons of the Afghan army.

What kind of foreign area expertise do these Soviet personnel in Afghanistan have? Do they speak Afghan languages and understand Afghan culture? Our discussion of research institutions outside Moscow described a large network of Asian study centers in the southern republics of the USSR.[99] Does the Soviet army use the expertise available at those centers to prepare officers to work in Afghanistan? These questions--perhaps not answerable at an unclassified level--also have to do with the effectiveness of Soviet military personnel working abroad.

Another major form of Soviet military interaction with Third World countries has emerged in the past 20 years: port visits by Soviet naval vessels. Admiral Gorshkov, commander-in-chief of the Soviet navy, explains what such port visits can accomplish:

> The friendly visits of Soviet sailors give the natives of the countries visited a chance to be convinced by their own eyes of the triumph of socialist principles in our country, the genuine equality of the peoples of the Soviet Union, and their high cultural level. Soviet sailors carry to the peoples of other countries the truth about our socialist country, our Soviet ideology and culture, and our Soviet way of life.[100]

We are not suggesting, of course, that Soviet sailors receive language and area training before being assigned to a ship operating in a particular region. The ship's political officers are more likely to receive such training.[101] Political officers arrange the "cultural exchange" aspects of port visits, such as shipboard movies and tours and "friendship meetings" between Soviet sailors and local citizens.

In other words, because political officers must serve as the Soviet navy's liaison with representatives of developing countries, we think it likely that they receive some training to prepare them for the job. However, once again we know little about how effective that training may be in making friends for the USSR.

In our view, this effectiveness issue is an important reason to examine more deeply the relationship between foreign area tasks and the skills of Soviet military personnel working abroad. The number of Soviet and Eastern European military technicians in the Third World has nearly quintupled in 15 years.[102] Soviet officers have taken control of the Afghan armed forces. Port visits by Soviet naval vessels are increasing. The Soviets are obviously investing great energy in showing their military power abroad.

We have little idea, however, about what kind of return the Soviets are receiving on their investment. If Soviet advisers are making fast friends in Africa because of their appreciation of local culture, that is one thing. If they are merely cementing a convenient marriage, that is another. Understanding which of the two situations really exists would help us to see more clearly the nature of the Soviet threat to U.S. interests in the developing world. Convenient marriages are easily thrown over, but fast friendships are not.

INTELLIGENCE SERVICES

The Committee for State Security and Main Intelligence Administration

The KGB combines the duties that both the CIA and FBI perform in the United States. It carries out intelligence missions abroad and keeps watch on both Soviet citizens and foreigners at home. The GRU (Soviet military intelligence) also conducts intelligence missions abroad—often parallel to those of the KGB—gathering intelligence useful to the Soviet armed forces. At home it is active in many organizations, but less so than the KGB. The GRU has long been considered the less powerful of the two agencies.

These two intelligence services pervade all dealings between the Soviet state and other countries. Students of the Soviet system, both insiders and outsiders, have written of this pervasiveness. For example, Oleg Penkovskiy, master spy and consummate insider, wrote in the early 1960s: "Anyone who has anything to do with the work of foreign countries, or who is connected with foreigners in the course of his work, is perforce engaged in intelligence work."[103]

Penkovskiy meant by this statement that every Soviet who works with foreigners may also be working for the KGB or GRU, because such individuals may be co-opted by these organizations when the need arises. A woman working in a shop that serves foreigners may be asked to note how much liquor a certain diplomat buys every week. A man escorting foreign trade delegations around Moscow may be asked to spot possible recruits for agent work. Neither of these people could be considered a full-time intelligence operative.

A large number of intelligence agents serve in Soviet missions abroad. Estimates of intelligence personnel among mission members range from 40 to 60 percent. The lower end of the scale, in our opinion, is closer to the truth.[104] In either case, the scope of Soviet intelligence activities abroad is clearly enormous.

Because KGB and GRU personnel participate in all Soviet dealings with foreigners, we may assume that the two intelligence services are the largest employers of foreign and double area specialists in the country. To the full-time intelligence officers must be added legions of specialists attached to other agencies, but co-opted by the services on a full- or part-time basis.

We regret that the constraints of time and security classification limit us to a somewhat cursory discussion of the internationalists' role in the KGB and GRU. However, we highlight several significant facts that illustrate the importance of such specialists to the Soviet intelligence sector.

The most stringent work for KGB and GRU officers, espionage abroad, involves two types of personnel: those who operate legally under Soviet diplomatic cover and those who disappear illegally into the societies to which they are assigned to live and work as locals. Both types are highly skilled professionals and members of an elite cadre.

Soviet intelligence operatives receive extensive language and area training. According to Harry Rositzke, "For twenty years the KGB has recruited the brightest young men, given them the most intensive language and area training, and converted them into 'specialists' (American, German, Latin American, even Turkish) by appropriate field assignments."[105]

Training differs according to the trainee's status at recruitment and final job assignment. For its U.S. operations, the KGB apparently recruits bright students who take part in Soviet-American academic exchanges. Some are tapped before they go to study in the United States, others when they return to the USSR. These students often have excellent English, many American acquaintances—especially in academic circles—and a firsthand knowledge of American life.[106]

The intelligence services, like other Soviet organizations employing foreign area specialists, put a premium on skills in unusual foreign
languages. A specialist is rotated among assignments slated to give him
the maximum exposure to the language and culture of his area. Furthermore, if the language is difficult, his salary may be adjusted upward to
compensate.

Rositzke reports that KGB officers in Iran were fluent in Farsi by
the early 1970s. Since Farsi is also the language spoken by the upper
classes in Afghanistan, these KGB Afghan-Iranian specialists have been
rotated with regularity between Teheran and Kabul. The knowledge of a
difficult language can bring a KGB employee as much as a 25 percent
salary increment.[107]

KGB officers under Soviet diplomatic cover turn up in developing
as well as developed countries. As accredited diplomats, they may engage in either espionage or establishing Soviet influence in the host
country. The latter is normally a job for diplomats. In the Soviet
case, however, it is also performed by KGB officers.

KGB agents working to establish Soviet influence spend their time
befriending local political leaders, government officials, and members
of the intelligentsia, using the opportunity to explain the Soviet view
of international controversies. They are well prepared for the task by
intensive language and area training. Furthermore, they are members of
an elite corps, well dressed, debonair, and equipped to impress the
locals. Finally, and perhaps most important, they are authorized to
meet with foreigners. The KGB must approve each person in the embassy
who meets routinely with foreigners, and its own officers are probably
first to gain such approval.

Covert, or clandestine, agents may also have good backgrounds and
educations before coming to the KGB or GRU. Their job assignments
differ from those of their overt colleagues, however, and their post-
recruitment training reflects this difference. One covert agent who
was caught was the highly educated son of a communist party *apparatchik*.
He had trained for eight years to become a facsimile of an American,
mastering American English and American mores and customs. He learned
welding, bookkeeping, and travel writing to give him flexibility in

choosing a stratum of American society in which to operate. He circulated among Americans in Moscow and Cairo to practice his skills and
lived for a time in Johannesburg to validate the background created for
him by the KGB.[108]

Apparently six or seven years is the average time needed to train
an illegal agent and build a false identity.[109] The KGB and GRU obviously consider the long-term commitment of manpower, facilities, and
resources to be worth the cost.

Once in the field, covert agents may engage in espionage or they
may disappear into a normal life and wait to be activated at some future
time. They are well enough trained in the host country's language and
peculiarities that they blend into its society with relative ease. They
are clearly the epitome of foreign area specialists.

The Soviet intelligence services also employ many foreign and
double area specialists inside the USSR. These employees work at KGB
or GRU headquarters in Moscow or in the many other government organizations that deal with foreign nations. Because we lack the time and
the resources to discuss all of the organizations in which intelligence
services place their employees in the Soviet system, we limit our discussion to the KGB, an intelligence agency, and the State Committee for
Science and Technology, a science policy agency with an important intelligence function.

How the KGB Uses Area and Double Area Specialists

The large KGB bureaucracy encompasses four chief directorates,
seven independent directorates, six independent departments, and numerous subdivisions. The First Chief Directorate, which is responsible
for Soviet espionage activities abroad, probably employs the largest
number of specialists with language and area training. Its functional
departments train illegal agents, acquire foreign technologies, process
information, penetrate foreign intelligence services, distribute disinformation, and arrange political murders and sabotage. According to
John Barron, however, "the greatest striking power of the First Chief
Directorate is concentrated in its ten geographic departments [which]
undertake a majority of the KGB enterprises abroad."[110]

The United States and Canada together rate one department in the First Chief Directorate and the Federal Republic of Germany and Austria another. The other eight departments are based on various regional groupings, e.g., the French-speaking nations of Africa. Each department is responsible for supervising, maintaining, and staffing the KGB residencies at embassies in its geographic area. It is also responsible for supporting clandestine agents in its territory.[111] Obviously, such activities require a large number of specialists with foreign language and area training.

The Second Chief Directorate keeps track of Soviet citizens and foreigners inside the USSR. Six of its departments, also divided along geographic lines, watch over foreign diplomats. Other functional departments concentrate on surveillance and recruitment of tourists, foreign students, and foreign journalists. The Second Chief Directorate thus also needs foreign and double area specialists, although perhaps fewer than the First.[112]

Many KGB and GRU jobs for which foreign area skills are needed show similarities to jobs in western intelligence services. Espionage work involving residence in a foreign country requires an intimate knowledge of that country, no matter who is doing the spying. Research jobs in the Soviet and western intelligence services differ, however, because western policymakers want analysis, whereas Soviet policymakers seem to prefer raw data.

In western intelligence services like the U.S. Central Intelligence Agency, a large cadre of analysts integrates information from many sources--human intelligence, open literature, electronic intelligence--and manipulates the data to separate out important facts. Given a problem, a CIA specialist may prepare an analysis based on conclusions reached after reviewing all sources of information available to him. He may even present policy recommendations along with his analysis. This analytic and policy-planning function is performed by a range of personnel from entry-level staff members to advisers in the director's office.

In the KGB, the Information Service of the First Chief Directorate would logically be expected to prepare the same kind of analysis from the same kinds of sources. Instead, it seems mainly to assemble raw data from these sources and distribute it to those with a "need to know," including top party leaders. These recipients apparently prefer to read unprocessed reports rather than finished intelligence analyses.[113]

This lack of analysis represents a long-standing preference on the part of the CPSU leadership. From its earliest days as a clandestine party, the CPSU has valued compartmentalization of information and secrecy. Even today, its leaders do not want intelligence data "filtered" by the lower echelons in the intelligence services. They prefer to make their own evaluations.

Evidence indicates, however, that the Politburo seeks a variety of inputs. Soviet leaders have never wanted centralized intelligence collection. Therefore, data flows to them from a number of sources, including the KGB, GRU, and Central Committee apparatus. Whatever analysis is done is probably done at the Central Committee level, but not in the form of massive studies. At the most, Central Committee International Department staff members prepare digests fusing intelligence data with policy choices. They are at the policymaking level; those in the intelligence services are not.[114]

Thus, intelligence jobs for foreign and double area specialists abound in the USSR. The KGB and GRU, however, use these specialists differently from the way in which they would be used by the western intelligence services. The most skilled specialists are probably considered more useful in the field, collecting information, than at home, evaluating it. An exception to this rule occurs in the area of science and technology.

How the State Committee for Science and Technology
Uses Area and Double Area Specialists

In the early 1960s, Oleg Penkovskiy described the intelligence functions of the State Committee for Coordination of Scientific Research Work, the predecessor of the GKNT. Penkovskiy, a GRU colonel, worked as a deputy section chief in the GKNT Directorate for Foreign Relations. The close relationship that he revealed between intelligence and the official mission of the GKNT conveys a sense of that relationship as it no doubt exists in most ministries having foreign dealings.

According to Penkovskiy, the GKNT was expanded in 1961, the greatest expansion taking place in the Directorate for Foreign Relations "to
improve the collection of scientific and technical intelligence information from the West by working with delegations from western states, as
well as by sending our own delegations of scientific specialists abroad
and organizing various exhibitions in foreign countries."[115]

As Penkovskiy described it, the main mission of the committee was
to coordinate the acquisition of technologies applicable to military
uses, not to coordinate research inside the USSR, as officially stated.
His day-to-day work involved keeping an eye on foreign scientific delegations, developing contacts among their members, and collecting industrial or technical data in any way that he could--personal contacts and
conversations, eavesdropping, searching baggage, even "stealing secrets
from visitors' pockets."[116] He was also responsible for screening Soviet scientists before they could travel abroad and for assigning members
of Soviet delegations the task of acquiring information during their
travels.

The GKNT today apparently continues many of these activities. John
Barron describes a close working relationship between the KGB's Scientific and Technical Directorate (in the First Chief Directorate) and the
GKNT. The S&T Directorate coordinates scientific, technical, and industrial espionage and determines which Soviet scientists may travel abroad.
The State Committee for Science and Technology, in conjunction with the
S&T Directorate, decides what needs can be met through espionage. This
task is part of its official mission to regulate and coordinate basic
research, dictate scientific priorities, and allocate resources.[117]

The GKNT, according to Barron, still employs many intelligence officers full time.[118] Because these officers decide how foreign technologies are important to the USSR, they provide an exception to the "no-
analysis" rule discussed above. They are specialists trusted to set
priorities and determine where Soviet interests lie in the various fields
of science and technology. Thus, except for employees of the Central
Committee departments, they are perhaps closer to the analysts in western
intelligence services than any other personnel in the Soviet system.

Although western observers take for granted the fact that the KGB and GRU pervade every government agency involved with foreigners, we do not want to convey the impression that these agencies engage in intelligence activities to the exclusion of their official missions. Penkovskiy conceded that his committee "has many different sections and directorates which work strictly in the field of the national economy."[119] Intelligence officers working at missions abroad, according to Rositzke, "must, for the most part, carry out their cover duties with reasonable efficiency. A UN official or a TASS correspondent has a job to do, and he cannot spend all his time away from his normal work."[120]

Furthermore, although we assume that intelligence work is part of every Soviet dealing with foreign nations, we cannot assume that it is the only activity of any importance to the Soviets. Commercial transactions, diplomacy, cultural exchange, among other activities, also play a part in Soviet international relations. Hence, the predictability of the relationship between the Soviet intelligence services and language and area specialists should not force us to lose sight of the other purposes for which their talents are used in the Soviet system.

Foreign and double area specialists in the USSR obviously do well to work for the KGB or GRU. These organizations offer important perquisites, including elite status and travel abroad, and hence they attract some of the best talent produced by the Soviet educational system. As specialists with language and area skills, young intelligence officers can expect to make excellent careers in the international field. For them as for many of their peers in other agencies, language and area skills are the key to interesting work, promotion, and success. A KGB or GRU officer can count on his foreign area expertise to advance his position and rank.[121]

MISSIONS ABROAD

The paucity of unclassified information on the operations of Soviet missions abroad is almost made up for by the vivid glimpse of those operations provided in the memoirs of Aleksandr Kaznacheev and Vladimir Sakharov.[122] Kaznacheev wrote about the late 1950s, when Soviet policymakers first began to realize the importance of the developing world. Sakharov wrote about the late 1960s and early 1970s, when the Soviet presence in the Third World had been fully established. Their accounts offer contrasts that highlight the role of Soviet foreign area specialists in missions abroad.

This section explores the two accounts, focusing on their differences, and augments them with information from other sources.[123] The discussion centers on the apparatus for conducting diplomacy and disbursing military and economic aid. Because it excludes intelligence-related and covert activities (indeed, most Soviet foreign missions seem connected to intelligence activities) the discussion is not an exhaustive review of Soviet missions abroad.

Each embassy apparently oversees, at least formally, an interlocking network of missions involved in aid programs, trade, propaganda, diplomacy, and intelligence. Despite this formal subordination, mission personnel report to their ministries in Moscow rather than directly to the ambassador, a bureaucratic double subordination that is often present in the Soviet system.[124]

According to Kaznacheev, Soviet foreign affairs specialists may be attached abroad to a trade mission under the Ministry of Foreign Trade, an economic mission of the State Committee for Economic Relations with Foreign Countries, a cultural mission under the State Committee for Cultural Relations with Foreign Countries, an information mission under the Soviet Information Bureau, or missions involving such Ministry of Foreign Trade organizations as Soviet Film Export or *Mezhkniga* (International Book). These missions are all outside the regular Ministry of Foreign Affairs structure.[125]

Kaznacheev notes also that TASS provides important positions for international journalists abroad.[126] Sakharov adds one more organization with which a Soviet foreign affairs specialist might find employment abroad: the International Department of the CPSU Central Committee.[127]

According to Kaznacheev, the trade mission was the largest group at the Soviet embassy in Burma in the late 1950s. Its efforts centered on "securing the Burmese market for Soviet manufactured goods, from soap to automobiles."[128]   Because of the poor reputation of Soviet goods in Burma, however, the mission's trade activities were less successful than its intelligence-related functions.   These included following Burma's economic relations with the West and penetrating local business circles.[129]

Furthermore, because the Burmese government hesitated to expand economic aid ties with Moscow, highly trained economists in the economic mission spent their time studying the Burmese economy.   The few technical aid specialists, e.g. construction engineers, in Burma were involved in only a limited number of projects.   They were accompanied on the job by interpreters.[130]

Sakharov paints a much different picture of Soviet aid personnel, based on his experience in the Middle East at the end of the 1960s.   He describes the unruly Soviet community of technicians who went straight from villages to work on projects in North Yemen and Egypt, unprepared for foreign service and untrained in Middle Eastern languages and culture.

Unable to control the brawling technicians, the Soviet diplomatic mission in Yemen assigned Sakharov the task of drawing up a list of those who got drunk and beat up their wives, because, according to his boss, "We must clean up this multinational gathering of degenerates we call Soviet road builders.   These people do everything to make us look bad, not only here but every country we bring them in."[131]

Sakharov blames this violence on poor planning from above.   For the first time, he says, Tadzhiks, Turkmens, Russians, Georgians, and Ukrainians were thrust together into a foreign environment where their age-old nationalistic animosities were exacerbated.   As a result of the Yemeni experience, the Central Committee from then on selected Soviet technicians for contracts abroad with an eye to their national backgrounds.[132]

The number of Soviet economic technicians in aid and trade programs in the Third World has expanded rapidly, increasing from 4,300 in 1960 to 33,000 in 1979.[133]   Hence, even if Soviet foreign technicians remain unacculturated, their government continues to send them abroad.

According to the CIA, trade between the USSR and less developed countries expanded rapidly because aid programs opened new markets for Soviet capital goods. The Soviets have focused on countries where they can obtain both political and economic advantage, such as raw materials for their manufacturing sectors. Expanded trade has meant large hard currency earnings, particularly since Soviet contractors raised the charges for the services of Soviet technicians abroad.[134]

Soviet foreign aid programs are the responsibility of the State Committee for Economic Relations with Foreign Countries. Both Kaznacheev and Sakharov describe GKES as an organization infiltrated by the Soviet intelligence services.[135] Nevertheless, it seems to fulfill a real foreign trade function apart from the Ministry of Foreign Trade. According to Triska and Finley, "Committee representatives oversee and coordinate foreign-trade-corporation personnel managers and technical specialists abroad in their work, setting up industrial enterprises and preparing local personnel for their operation and management."[136]

Soviet foreign affairs specialists apparently fill a variety of GKES positions abroad. For example, a specialist may work in one of the eleven GKES all-union associations (V/O),[137] which provide technical aid and equipment for everything from nuclear power plants to agricultural enterprises. Or, he may work in the Treaty, Protocol, and Legal Department of the Main Engineering Administration of GKES, negotiating technical assistance agreements with Third World clients.

The following list of GKES departments shows many other possibilities for employment abroad.[138]

Main Administration for Deliveries

Main Engineering Administration
  Aviation Supplies Department
  Treaty, Protocol, and Legal Department

Main Technical Administration

Main Department of Supplies

Department of Construction of Enterprises Abroad

Finance Department

Department for Latin America and West Africa

Legal Department

Department for the Near and Middle East

Department of Planning and Construction

Planning and Economics Department

Protocol Department

Department for Socialist Countries

Economic and Technical Cooperation with Mongolian
People's Republic

V/O Atomenergoeksport (exports and imports nuclear power
plants and equipment)

V/O Neftekhimpromeksport (exports complete installations
for petroleum and chemical enterprises)

V/O Prommasheksport (provides aid and equipment for me-
chanical engineering enterprises)

V/O Sel'khozpromeksport (supplies aid to agricultural
enterprises)

V/O Tekhnoeksport (supplies aid and equipment for civil
engineering and cultural projects)

V/O Tekhnopromeksport (provides aid to electric power
installations)

V/O Tekhnostroyeksport (handles construction projects
abroad, including design and equipment procurement)

V/O Tekhvneshreklama (advertising)

V/O Tekhvneshtrans (handles foreign trade transport operations connected with Soviet technical assistance in
setting up and operating industrial enterprises and
other projects abroad)

V/O Tsvetmetpromeksport (provides technical assistance
in building nonferrous metal, coal, and gas enterprises;
oil pipelines; and other projects abroad)

V/O Tyazhpromeksport (provides aid in constructing steel,
mining, coal, and oil industry enterprises)

Both Kaznacheev and Sakharov report a broad spectrum of embassy
activities under the heading of cultural relations. They also write
that these activities have intelligence as well as propaganda functions.
Kaznacheev states, for example, that the cultural mission at the embassy
in Burma organized exhibits, tours by Soviet performing groups, and the
supply of Soviet films and literature to Burmese political groups. "The
wide range of cultural efforts," he says, "provided an excellent cover

for Intelligence activities, which in fact were the main purpose of the mission's existence."[139] The commercial firm Soviet Film Export was also largely devoted to intelligence activities; *Mezhkniga* and the Soviet Information Bureau were more involved in disinformation and propaganda.[140]

Sakharov wrote that the Soviet cultural center in Alexandria, where his wife taught Russian, was like all Soviet cultural centers abroad, headed by a KGB officer. "Its prime task was to screen potential KGB candidates from those who visited the center."[141]

Although it seems clear that Soviet cultural missions are intimately involved with the intelligence services, they also perform other important functions that require the skills of specialists trained in languages and foreign cultures, and willing to work abroad. Natasha Sakharova's job teaching Russian in the Alexandria cultural center is a good example.[142]

The State Committee for Cultural Relations with Foreign Countries, which oversees cultural missions in Soviet embassies, also employs many foreign area specialists. According to Triska and Finley, the committee handles academic and theatrical exchanges with capitalist countries and organizes cultural exchange exhibits. In the developing countries, it also "promotes and oversees a wide variety of programs running from the export of doctors and medical facilities to needy countries, through jointly undertaken scientific research expeditions and projects, to the importation of students for all sorts of technical education and training in the USSR."[143]

Sakharov recounts that a representative of the CPSU Central Committee's International Department exerted great authority in Cairo, overriding even the KGB. The party official was able to co-opt all of Sakharov's time for work on a high-priority propaganda campaign, depriving the KGB and MFA of their best Arabist in Egypt.[144]

The International Department now has its own representatives in many Soviet embassies abroad, a process that began with Brezhnev's ascension to power. These representatives apparently report not to the Soviet ambassador but directly to Moscow through their own channels.[145]

According to Leonard Shapiro, the International Department representatives also "collect information about political parties and groupings, assess the political situation of the country concerned, and establish contacts with progressive organizations and individuals."[146] Sakharov's experience confirms this assessment.

In short, International Department representatives are the cream of Soviet foreign affairs specialists serving abroad. Although they usually serve as counselors or first secretaries of the embassy, their power is much greater than their rank implies; neither the ambassador nor the KGB may interfere in their business.

Unlike the Soviet road builders, military advisers serving in Third World countries in Sakharov's time presented no problem.[147] These military advisers have become both more numerous and more profitable to the Soviets in recent years. Whereas in the 1950s and 1960s the USSR was known as a supplier of outmoded if low-cost weaponry, in the 1970s it began to offer its Third World clients the latest that its arsenals could provide.[148]

Modern military equipment requires extensive training in maintenance and operation, and the demand has grown for Soviet and East European military advisers to work in developing countries. We do not know whether military technicians receive any special language or area training before leaving the USSR for their Third World assignments. The CIA notes that Third World countries have at times objected to heavy-handed Soviet methods,[149] implying that the advisers have no great understanding of the cultures in which they operate. However, the CIA also notes that the list of Soviet arms customers keeps growing.

International institutions comprise another category in which Soviet foreign affairs specialists can serve abroad. The largest number serve in United Nations organizations, including UNESCO, the International Labor Organization, the Economic Commissions for Europe and the Far East, and the International Atomic Energy Agency.[150]

The USSR also enjoys the benefits of three delegations to the United Nations: the Soviet, Ukrainian, and Belorussian.[151] Since the latter two have never deviated from the Soviet position at the UN, it appears that the delegations provide additional slots abroad for *Soviet* foreign affairs specialists--not simply for Ukrainians and Belorussians.

Some opportunities to serve in missions abroad in the Soviet system receive less attention than the usual diplomatic, economic, and cultural posts. For example, the USSR Ministry of Fisheries stations specialists in foreign embassies. Two fisheries attaches at the Soviet embassy in Washington handle day-to-day matters involving the Soviet fishing fleet off U.S. shores, including emergency medical evacuations from Soviet vessels. They also maintain contacts in U.S. government departments and on Capitol Hill.[152]

Beside the full-time KGB and GRU operatives who work either in the field or behind desks at embassies, many mission members whose official duties lie elsewhere devote at least part of their time to intelligence. The defection of Arkady N. Shevchenko in April 1978 widely publicized the intelligence duties of the Soviet United Nations delegations.[153] However, the vigorous diplomatic, economic, and cultural efforts that the Soviets pursue around the world indicate that an embassy staff's entire effort is not spent on intelligence.

In addition to intelligence, therefore, tasks abound for all kinds of specialists with foreign language and area skills. We unfortunately know little about whether such personnel as aid technicians receive special training. We know, however, that many staff members of Soviet missions abroad are highly skilled specialists able to operate easily in the country to which they are assigned.

COMMERCIAL ENTERPRISES

In recent years, the USSR's economic interaction with the non-Communist world has grown steadily in scope and volume. It stands to reason--and whatever information we have confirms--that the large and diversified administrative apparatus supporting these activities constitutes a major area of international specialist employment. We found such specialists serving in relevant ministries; ad hoc and permanent trade missions; agencies and committees concerned with commercial exports and imports, technology transfer, and economic assistance programs; Soviet commercial and technical subsidiaries operating in foreign

countries; and the small but growing number of joint Soviet-foreign
firms.

This listing of the principal categories of international specialist employment in the economic sphere suggests the diversity of current
Soviet external economic activities and the multiplicity of relevant
organizations that need to be studied for any assessment of this sector's relative significance as a source of employment for Soviet international affairs specialists. Because of limited time and resources,
we were forced to limit our research to a cursory examination of the
more readily available documentary materials.

Given larger resources, an in-depth study of the subject could
fill a good many now existing gaps in our knowledge. Such a study would
have to include a systematic review of (1) the large body of documentation issued by U.S. and foreign government agencies and (2) statistical
and descriptive information contained in Soviet sources other than the
most obvious ones used for this report. Valuable information could also
be extracted from the reports of non-Soviet business firms and academic
research institutes. The several specialized Soviet studies and non-
Soviet periodic publications concerned with the trade and commerce of
the USSR could also help to fill gaps in our information.[154]

What follows then constitutes no more than a quick and necessarily
fragmentary identification of major, not previously discussed, aspects
of Soviet international economic activity where specialists in international affairs or individuals with foreign language and area training
find useful employment. Whatever statistical data we present are intended only for illustrative purposes. At this stage in our research,
scholarly caution dictates that we refrain from attempting even a rough
estimate of the total number of Soviet international specialists now
active in the vast Soviet bureaucratic apparatus responsible for the
administration and development of economic and technical interaction
abroad.

In the past decade, Soviet trade has increased fourfold, from 10.1
billion rubles in 1960 to 22.1 billion in 1970, 50.7 billion in 1975,
and 80.3 billion in 1979.[155] Short of major changes in the international situation, the USSR appears bent on continuing to develop its

foreign economic ties with the industrialized West and with the developing nations, while pursuing its goal of economically integrating countries already under its political-military control.

The Soviet government assigns great importance to the expansion of
its foreign economic relations. The guidelines for Soviet economic and
social development in the 1980s adopted by the 26th CPSU Congress in
February 1981 stressed the need to further expand trade and economic,
scientific, and technical cooperation with foreign countries. This
task obviously requires a corps of international specialists familiar
with conditions abroad.

Prospects for increasing use of well-trained international specialists are also enhanced by the ever-growing number, geographic spread,
and diversity of economic systems and policies of Soviet trading partners. Official 1979 Soviet statistics put the total of Soviet trading
partners variously at around 100.[156]

Today, the USSR probably has economic ties with well over 100 foreign nations. A recent article in the authoritative *Ekonomicheskaya
gazeta* stated that in 1979 the USSR traded with 86 developing nations.[157] Adding other nations, one arrives at a minimum total of 110
countries, about the same number in which the USSR currently maintains
embassies.[158]

The Ministry of Foreign Trade operates a large bureaucracy staffed
with experts, including a substantial number of specialists in international economics and foreign market analysis, many with expertise on
particular countries.[159] Permanent trade missions in the major nations
serve as its instruments abroad.[160] Increasingly, however, these permanent representations are being supplemented by short-term survey or
negotiating teams. These may take the form of purchasing missions that
travel to the West to negotiate large-scale deals that cannot be handled
by the embassies' permanent trading missions. In some cases the negoti-
ations are sufficiently important, complex, and time-consuming to lead
to the establishment of temporary purchasing offices staffed by Soviet
personnel.[161]

As in other areas involving Soviet delegations sent abroad, reliable information regarding the staffing patterns of such missions and

teams is lacking. Apparently they are made up primarily of economic
and technical experts, but include also specialists familiar with political and market conditions in the particular foreign country, as well
as with its administrative-organizational structure and procedures.
They may operate on temporary assignment out of their Moscow home offices or in some instances be assigned abroad for extended periods or
semipermanently.[162]

The USSR has long operated sales and representational offices in
the territories of its major trading partners. Best known among these
are Soviet banking enterprises (e.g., Narodnyy Bank), tourist agencies
(e.g., *Intourist*), news agencies (e.g., TASS), and transportation companies. Among the larger employers in the latter category is Aeroflot,
the Soviet airline, which maintains offices all over the world to support its operations.

In each of the 86 countries it serves,[163] Aeroflot routinely keeps
its own ticketing agents and maintenance crews, rather than hiring local personnel as many large international carriers do. The USSR's
international air carrier, in other words, employs a large number of
Soviet citizens abroad.

Of course, often the number of people required to staff an Aeroflot
operation is limited by the facilities available in a host country. For
example, ticketing agents in the United States use U.S. computers, and
ground crews use U.S. maintenance equipment. Thus, Soviet computer and
equipment specialists are not needed in the United States.

When the Soviet government approaches a developing country about
establishing Aeroflot service, however, the offer is frequently an extensive package deal. According to Ralph Ostrich of the BDM Corporation, the deal may include ticketing and maintenance staffs as well as
personnel to operate and service sophisticated ground control approach
equipment, which the Soviets also provide.[164] Thus, although the Aeroflot staff in the United States is limited, in a less developed country
it may be large, diverse, and capable of handling a variety of sophisticated machines.

We do not know precisely how much language and area training Aeroflot employees receive before they are sent abroad. It seems likely

that personnel in ticket offices are recruited from universities and institutes where they acquired three or four languages. They probably also are instructed in or have prior knowledge of rudimentary international economic principles, such as how to compute monetary exchange rates. Furthermore, air controllers working at Third World airports where Aeroflot is not the only traffic almost certainly speak English, and perhaps French, Portuguese, or Spanish.

However, ground crews and other maintenance staff may have very little language or area training. This is an issue that deserves further investigation, for if such personnel are forced by lack of language capability to live in isolation in their host countries, their utility to the Soviet government in areas such as intelligence gathering may be limited. On the other hand, if they have language and area training, they probably provide excellent service in a large number of countries.

Even a cursory study of the available information on Soviet foreign trade with the industrialized nations points to an interesting phenomenon suggesting Soviet efforts to reconcile central direction from Moscow (and Marxist-Leninist theory) with the requirements of operations in the capitalist West. Indications of growing experimentation in that regard can be seen in the rather unexpected appearance of Soviet mixed equity companies in the industrial countries. The present situation is best summarized by a quotation from McMillan's detailed study:

> Traditionally, socialist foreign commerce has been conducted abroad through official trade delegations or through foreign agency companies. Wholly owned trading companies abroad (such as Amtorg Trading Corporation in the United States) have been the exception. More recently, socialist foreign trade enterprises and other economic organizations have increasingly found it necessary not only to open their own representational offices abroad but also to establish branches or to form subsidiary companies (most often with local partners) in order to engage directly in a widening variety of business activities.[165]

McMillan found that by March 1979 the USSR had equity in 117 foreign companies. Some 92 of these companies were located in 17 western industrialized countries and another 25 in 19 developing countries. Most of the firms in the industrialized countries were involved in trading and marketing, although some concentrated on manufacturing, natural resource exploitation, or financial, commercial and engineering services.[166]

The Soviets seemingly prefer to maintain operational control of foreign companies that they wholly or partly own. Often, Soviet nationals work as top managers of enterprises based abroad, and foreign nationals work as their employees. In other cases, Soviet and foreign nationals are equal partners in the firm and share its operational control.

A U.S.-Soviet joint venture, Marine Resources of Seattle, Washington, is jointly operated. The firm was incorporated in 1976 to catch, process, and market fish cooperatively on the west coast of the United States. Each of the participants—Sovrybflot, an agency of the Soviet Ministry of Fisheries, and Bellingham Cold Storage of Bellingham, Washington—holds 50 percent of the company's capital stock.

The top management of the Marine Resources Seattle headquarters consists of an American president and one Soviet and one American vice-president. The firm's second office in Nakhodka, USSR, has two directors, one Soviet and one American. One U.S. newspaper called Marine Resources "the model joint venture," and the *Nakhodkinskiy rabochiy* (Nakhodka Worker) lauded the close cooperation of the partners even in times of international tension.[167]

Soviets directing enterprises abroad are generally permanent employees of the parent organization in the USSR. They can expect to spend at least one extended tour abroad and may in the course of a career work in several foreign countries. As a result, they become experienced international businessmen. In the Ministry of Foreign Trade, which indirectly oversees most Soviet foreign subsidiaries, a senior official may typically have worked abroad as the director of an enterprise, moved up to head a trade mission, and then returned to Moscow as a division chief in the ministry.[168]

Below the management level, most employees of Soviet companies abroad tend to be citizens of the host country. Thus, while the Soviets apparently prefer to maintain operational control of their foreign subsidiaries, they are not opposed to the cost-saving practice of hiring staff locally.

Practically speaking, those two tendencies reflect the evidence
that Soviet companies abroad do not behave "significantly differently
from western foreign subsidiary companies."[169] In other words, the
Soviets possess a top echelon of international businessmen, highly
trained in western practices, who run their foreign-based companies
very much as their western counterparts do. One element of their operating procedures must be efficiency and cost-saving in personnel practices, and for that reason, they hire foreign nationals for lower level
jobs.

Soviet foreign trade specialists working abroad, therefore, would
probably tend to be just that--foreign trade specialists. Double area
specialists would be much less in evidence, except at the highest level
of technical adviser. Hence, the Finnish owner of a Soviet car would
not bring it to a Soviet mechanic to be serviced. Instead, the local
dealership would employ Finnish mechanics, Finnish salesmen, and probably a Finnish manager. However, the manager's boss in Helsinki would
likely be a Soviet.

Inside the USSR, the Soviets pursue forms of commercial cooperation much different from their joint equity companies abroad. Apparently, the vision of Toyota building, operating, and maintaining control of an automobile plant in Minsk remains unattractive to Soviet
leaders. They allow instead five different types of cooperative ventures, all of which permit Soviet enterprises to maintain some level of
control over operations:

1. Licensing with payment in product. The western partner
    provides either licenses, or licenses, know-how, and
    parts. The Soviet partner repays with the finished
    product.
2. Turnkey with payment in product. The western partner
    provides the turnkey plant; the Soviet partner repays
    with the finished product.
3. Coproduction and specialization. Each partner special-
    izes in the production of certain parts of a final
    product or in the production of a limited number of
    items in a manufacturing program.

4. Subcontracting. The western partner takes advantage of presumed lower wage costs in the socialist partner states.

5. Joint tendering or joint projects. These usually involve partner collaboration in third countries, but can also serve as a mechanism for joint venture arrangements otherwise illegal in the USSR.[170]

Because they were designed to keep Soviets in control, each of these forms of cooperation provides potential employment for Soviet foreign area specialists. For example, a turnkey project usually involves a long-term relationship with the foreign partner, perhaps involving updates in plant technology over time. Thus, the Soviet plant managers probably have to employ staff capable of serving as liaison with their western counterparts more or less on a permanent basis.

These few examples suggest the scope and diversity of Soviet economic involvement with foreign countries. International specialists obviously have ample opportunity to find employment in this area of Soviet external activity. Having said this, we must admit that only much greater attention to their role than we have been able to accord it could fill the large gaps in our knowledge of their functions within the Soviet system.

INTERNATIONAL EXCHANGES

This section describes Soviet organizations involved in international exchanges other than those already covered above.[171] The scope and variety of these exchange activities conveys a sense of the many positions in exchange administration to be filled by foreign area specialists.

In April 1981, the USSR signed agreements on cultural and scientific exchanges with Ecuador and Morocco and on cooperation in filmmaking with Nicaragua.[172] Around the world, the Soviets have entered into agreements for cooperation in areas as diverse as fisheries, industrial development, science, education, and culture. Because we have the most information about Soviet cooperation agreements with the United States,

we will concentrate on these. Note, however, that all U.S. government-sponsored exchanges ceased in 1980, after the Soviets invaded
Afghanistan.

Academia is the best-established area of Soviet-American exchange
cooperation. Scholars began traveling between the two countries in
1956-1957, and the procedure became formalized with the signing of the
Soviet-American Exchange Agreement in 1958. The International Research and Exchanges Board (IREX) took over administration of the exchanges on the American side in 1969; on the Soviet side it has been
handled by foreign relations offices of the Ministry of Higher and Specialized Secondary Education and the USSR Academy of Sciences.[173]

The State Committee for Science and Technology administers Soviet
science and technology exchange agreements. The United States and USSR
have 11 intergovernmental agreements in science and technology. American industrial firms may also conclude cooperation agreements with the
Soviets; on the Soviet side, these are also handled by the State Committee for Science and Technology.[174] In addition, the USSR Academy of
Sciences and the U.S. National Academy of Sciences, a private institution chartered by the U.S. government, conduct their own scientific
exchanges.[175]

Cultural cooperation has been an important part of the Soviet-
American relationship since the original exchange agreement of 1958.
The United States and USSR have exchanged cultural exhibits almost every
year. American exhibits traveling in the USSR have been shepherded
from city to city by representatives of the Soviet Chamber of Commerce,
which also sponsors trade fairs in the USSR. Although the representatives may not be English speakers themselves, they are always accompanied by Chamber of Commerce translators.

Cultural exchanges have also included dance, music, and vocal con-
certs by performers ranging from rock stars to prima ballerinas. On
the Soviet side, these exchanges are administered under the Ministry of
Culture by *Goskontsert*, the State Concert Association of the USSR.

Goskontsert serves as both commercial manager for Soviet artists
performing in the West and government cultural exchange agency for
western artists performing in the USSR. This dual role came about

because Soviet artists want to earn U.S. dollars, but American artists
are unwilling to be paid in rubles, which they cannot spend outside the
USSR and cannot exchange for hard currency. As a result, Soviet artists perform in the U.S. on commercial concert tours arranged by *Goskontsert* and U.S. impresarios like Sol Hurok. American artists perform
in the USSR on cultural exchange tours arranged by *Goskontsert* and the
U.S. International Communications Agency. Both groups of artists earn
U.S. dollars.

Goskontsert needs specialists familiar with the operations of western concert managers, the nuances of cultural exchange agreements, and
the operations of government cultural exchange agencies abroad. *Goskontsert* likely divides the responsibilities of its staff geographically,
at least to some extent. We know, for example, that it employs at least
one consultant on U.S. affairs.[176]

The various propaganda and foreign friendship organizations[177] have
an important cultural exchange function which they seem well designed to
perform. The Union of Soviet Societies for Friendship and Cultural Relations with Foreign Countries, for example, has at least six functional
departments to deal with agriculture, social science, law, theater, and
architecture. It also has geographic departments. Finally, it administers close to 60 friendship societies, which are organized between the
USSR and individual or groups of countries.

Some of these societies have branches in the USSR. The USSR-USA
Society, for example, has a branch in Leningrad; the Soviet-Vietnam
Friendship Society has a branch in Vladivostok.[178] In short, the Union
of Friendship Societies is an extensive bureaucracy providing many job
opportunities for foreign area specialists.

Other forms of Soviet-American exchange cooperation include university-to-university exchanges, such as those between Moscow State University and the State University of New York; language study programs,
such as that sponsored by the Council for International Educational Exchange and Leningrad State University; foreign policy seminars, such as
those sponsored by the U.S. and Soviet United Nations Associations; and
citizen group exchanges, such as those organized by the Citizens' Exchange Corps.[179] All of these exchanges are administered by

organizations in the USSR that employ staff who have at least foreign
language skills. Many probably also have area specializations.

Numerous organizations as diverse as the State Committee for Science and Technology, the Ministry of Culture, and the State Universities in Moscow and Leningrad engage in foreign exchanges. These exchanges, all administered by agencies of the Soviet government, require
large numbers of linguists, area specialists, and dual area specialists
to carry them out.

Section III Notes

1. *Narodnoye khozyaystvo SSSR v 1978 g.* (Statistical Yearbook of the USSR--1978), Izdatel'stvo Statistika, Moscow, 1979, p. 466.

2. Ibid., p. 470. These figures include only those teaching in grades four through ten and eleven.

3. Z. Verdiyeva, "Nravstvennaya gran' vysshey shkoly" (The Moral Side of Higher School), *Kommunist*, No. 14, September 1980, p. 68.

4. Ibid.

5. Ibid., p. 69.

6. Ibid., p. 71.

7. Ibid., p. 74.

8. The phenomenon of the convenient marriage (*fiktivnyy brak*) apparently appears in many sectors of Soviet society, and for many reasons. For example, because travel abroad is often limited to those with families to leave behind, an academic who wants to go to the United States may arrange a *fiktivnyy brak* so as to obtain permission to go.

9. Steven A. Grant, *Soviet Americanists*, International Communications Agency, Office of Research, R-1-80, February 15, 1980, p. 2. (Hereafter cited as *Soviet Americanists.*)

10. Ibid., pp. 4-5.

11. Ibid., p. 6.

12. Ibid. and interview with Steven Grant.

13. *Soviet Americanists*, p. 6.

14. Oded Eran, *The Mezhdunarodniki--An Assessment of Professional Expertise in the Making of Soviet Foreign Policy*, Turtledove Publishing, Ramat Gan, Israel, 1979, p. 257.

15. Interview with Mark Kuchment.

16. Seymour M. Rosen, *Soviet Programs in International Education*, U.S. Department of Health, Education, and Welfare, (OE)75-19115, November 1974, p. 8.

17. Ibid., p. 7.

18. Ibid. A description of typical graduate students and researchers who participated in the exchanges appears on p. 14.

19. International Research and Exchanges Board (IREX), *Annual Report, 1976-1977*, and *1977-1978*, New York, pp. 47-49 and 55-57.

20. We thank Dr. Valentina Golondzowski-Brougher for her recollections of Soviet exchange groups based at Georgetown University, Washington, D.C.

21. Rosen, p. 6.

22. Ibid.

23. Ibid., p. 10.

24. Ibid.

25. For the organization and functions of the R&D-related efforts in the Academy's institutes, see Simon Kassel and Cathleen Campbell, *The Soviet Academy of Sciences and Technological Development*, The Rand Corporation, R-2533-ARPA, December 1980.

26. *Narodnoye khozyaystvo SSSR v 1979 g.* (Statistical Yearbook of the USSR--1979), Izdatel'stvo Statistika, Moscow, 1980, p. 109. That source provides only the total number of academicians. William F. and Harriet Scott give the number of full members in 1978 as 235 and of corresponding members as 477; see "The Social Sciences Institutes of the Soviet Academy of Sciences," *Air Force Magazine*, March 1980.

27. *Narodnoye khozyaystvo SSSR v 1979 g.*, the most recent available statistical handbook, gives the exact number as 46,115 (p. 109).

28. This is also the title of Oded Eran's book, cited in note 14; the book has been helpful in the preparation of this section.

29. See, for example, Nora Beloff, "Escape from Boredom--A Defector's Story," *Atlantic Monthly*, November 1980. The article is based on interviews with Galina Orionova, described as a former research fellow or assistant of IUSAC. According to Beloff, Orionova contended that except for Arbatov, the director of IUSAC, "nobody in the Institute has the remotest connection with the government" (p. 44), that "the Institute has not the slightest impact on Soviet foreign policy" (ibid.), and that "only Arbatov, who is a candidate member (i.e., member without voting rights) of the Central Committee, ever had access to policy-makers. Between 1971 and 1975 he was so busy with government affairs we hardly saw him. When detente declined he came back." (Arbatov has since been raised to full membership in the Central Committee.) Orionova's point is that the institute has no influence on policy but that its propaganda function is generally underestimated. While we cannot cover every aspect of this controversy, we would like to point out that it is unlikely that any simple researcher on the IUSAC staff enjoys direct access to those who wield power in the Soviet system. On the other hand, Arbatov indisputably had such access to Brezhnev and other key figures. To what extent his opinions are taken into account is beyond our knowledge, but at least he is consulted. In turn, he is not a figurehead at IUSAC (for example, Orionova was personally interviewed by him), and the results of his staff's research no doubt are reflected in his judgments regarding U.S. conditions, policies, intentions, and capabilities.

30. Anatoliy Gromyko, now known as an Africa specialist, served in diplomatic posts in the United States and wrote the first Soviet book-length study of the workings of the U.S. Congress.

31. For more on the old boy network among key institute personnel who are graduates of MGIMO, see p. 25.

32. *Pravda*, October 11, 1980, p. 3.

33. Formal and informal means of party and government control over the Academy and its subsidiary research institutions would at any rate be sufficiently effective to prevent the publication of findings in open contradiction to official policy positions or interpretations. The Academy is under the direct control of the Council of Ministers, which in turn is guided by the CPSU Central Committee. The institutes must conduct their research and select research topics in accordance with annual research plans that must have the approval of the higher administrative echelons. Scientific councils and other coordinating mechanisms also serve as controls. These councils include both staff members of the interested research institutes and representatives of party and government. In August 1973, for example, the Social Science Division of the Academy set up, in accordance with an Academy Presidium resolution, a Scientific Council for [the study of] U.S. Economic, Political, and Ideological Problems to determine the main avenues of research activity in the field of Soviet-U.S. studies.

34. See Blair A. Ruble, *Soviet Research Institutes Project, Volume I: The Policy Sciences*, United States Information Agency, Office of Research, R-5-81, February 19, 1981, pp. 379-380. (Hereafter cited as *Soviet Research Institutes Report, Vol. I*.)

35. The trend has led to a stepped-up monitoring and translating effort in areas hitherto largely neglected. Within a year after its establishment, the new institute was monitoring over 110 American periodicals. See Richard F. Vidmer, "Management Science in the USSR--The Role of 'Americanizers,'" *International Studies Quarterly*, Vol. 24, No. 3, September 1980, p. 409.

36. Few organizations in the USSR are *not* government-sponsored. For the purpose of this discussion, however, "government" will refer to ministries, state committees, and other entities having functional missions that would benefit from applied research. "Academic" will refer to teaching and research organizations oriented toward the theoretical.

37. For more on GKES, see pp. 108-109.

38. *Communist Aid Activities in Non-Communist Less Developed Countries, 1979 and 1954-79*, Central Intelligence Agency, ER 80-10318U, October 1980, pp. 2, 8.

39. *Soviet Research Institutes Report, Vol. I*, p. 85.

40. Ibid.

41. This discussion touches on a point that we will expand in our conclusions. For information on the MGU laboratory, see Mark H. Teeter et al., *Soviet Research Institutes Project, Volume III: The Humanities*, United States Information Agency, Office of Research, July 1981, p. 294. (Hereafter cited as *Soviet Research Institutes Report, Vol. III*.) See also *Soviet Americanists*, p. 6. For more on the Oriental Faculty at Leningrad, see *Soviet Research Institutes Report, Vol. I*, pp. 406-408; on the group at Kiev, see ibid., pp. 379-380, 415.

42. Ibid., p. 416.

43. Ibid., pp. 388-391, 410, 416.

44. Grant notes that individual researchers around the country publish articles on America, but do not seem part of any large-scale *amerikanistika* programs. See *Soviet Americanists*, fn 6. Ruble states that Gor'kiy State University, with a dozen specialists in American affairs, "ranks among the more active university American studies centers in the USSR today." *Soviet Research Institutes Report, Vol. I*, p. 402. As is evident from our earlier discussion, a variety of foreign languages are taught at universities and institutes throughout the USSR. However, most of these could probably not be considered full-fledged research organizations devoted to linguistics or philology.

45. This table is derived from *Soviet Research Institutes Report, Vol. I*, pp. 402-418. For more detailed information on the institutes, see those pages.

46. The ranks of foreign area specialists not directly associated with the media but frequently lending their expertise to them include Academician Evgeniy Primakov, a leading Arabist who heads the Institute of Oriental Studies of the USSR Academy of Sciences; Dr. Anatoliy Gromyko, Director of the Academy's African Institute; Dr. I. Latyshev, now active in the academic world after years of journalistic activity in Tokyo; and Dr. Ivan I. Kovalenko, section chief in the International Department of the CPSU Central Committee, a party official with substantial Japanese linguistic competence and experience in Japanese affairs.

47. See Jan F. Triska and David D. Finley, "The Institutions of Soviet Foreign Policy," *Soviet Foreign Policy*, The Macmillan Co., New York, 1968, p. 45.

48. See, for example, John L. Scherer (ed.), *USSR Facts and Figures Annual*, Vol. 4, 1980, p. 337. He points out that Brezhnev's daughter, Galina, is a high official of the Novosti news agency; her brother, Mikhail Brezhnev, is studying journalism at Moscow University; the late Premier Aleksey Kosygin's daughter, Lyudmila, who majored in English, serves as a senior researcher in the Institute of Scientific Information; Kosygin's second daughter heads the All-Union Library for Foreign Literature.

49. Ibid., pp. 225-226.

50. *The Europa Year Book 1980*, Vol. 1, London, 1980, p. 1265, and *USSR Facts and Figures Annual*, 1980, p. 292. The latter draws for its information on *Moscow News*. According to the Soviet media handbook *Pechat' SSSR v 1979 godu*, Moscow, 1980, the total number of Soviet newspapers in 1979 was 8019. Presumably the papers not receiving the TASS news service are of limited circulation or specialize in matters where international affairs are not directly relevant.

51. CIA study quoted in U.S. Congress, House, *Hearings before the Subcommittee of the Permanent Select Committee on Intelligence*, 95th Cong., 1st and 2d sess., December 27, 1977-April 20, 1978. Information obtained from a private American press source corroborates that figure.

52. Interview with Sergey Losev: "Increasing the Quality and Rapidity of Information Is the Main Thing," *Zhurnalist*, No. 4, April 1981, translated in Joint Publications Research Service (JPRS), *USSR Report*, Political and Sociological Affairs, JPRS 78566, July 21, 1981, p. 29.

53. Triska and Finley, p. 45.

54. "The Propaganda Sweepstakes," *Time*, March 9, 1981.

55. The geographic spread of these expanding associations is evident from occasional TASS dispatches. The agency reported on October 24, 1980, that it had concluded an exchange-of-information agreement with the Italian news agency Italia; three weeks later it reported from Moscow that it had signed a similar understanding with the Nicaraguan news agency Nueva Nicaragua. See Foreign Broadcast Information Service (FBIS), *Daily Report--USSR*, November 12 and 17, 1980.

56. Ibid.

57. *The Europa Year Book 1980*, Vol. 1, p. 1265.

58. CIA study quoted in U.S. Congress, House, *Hearings before the Subcommittee of the Permanent Select Committee on Intelligence.*

59. Ibid.

60. Rand has published the following studies on the role of the media in intraelite communication in Eastern Europe: Jane Leftwich Curry and A. Ross Johnson, *The Media and Intra-Elite Communication in Poland* (Summary Report), R-2627, December 1980; Lilita Dzirkals, Thane Gustafson, and A. Ross Johnson, *The Media and Intra-Elite Communication in the USSR*, R-2869, forthcoming; Jane Leftwich Curry, *The Media and Intra-Elite Communication in Poland: Organization and Control of the Media*, N-1514/1, December 1980; Jane Leftwich Curry, *The Media and Intra-Elite Communication in Poland: The System of Censorship*, N-1514/2, December 1980; A. Ross Johnson, *The Media and Intra-Elite Communication in Poland: The Role of Military Journals*, N-1514/3, December 1980; Jane Leftwich Curry, *The Media and Intra-Elite Communication in Poland: The Role of "Special Bulletins,"* N-1514/4, December 1980; Jane Leftwich Curry and A. Ross Johnson, *The Media and Intra-Elite Communication in Poland: Case Studies of Controversy*, N-1514/5, December 1980.

61. Our survey used both Soviet and non-Soviet bibliographic works; *Pechat' SSSR v 1979 godu* and *Knizhnaya letopis'* proved especially useful, as did *USSR Facts and Figures Annual, 1980*, which draws on a variety of Soviet and other sources. Our figures are based on Soviet statistics, which often use different definitions from those normally employed in U.S. compilations. Thus, "titles" includes books as well as pamphlets and reprints.

62. Eric Morgenthaler, *Wall Street Journal*, February 21, 1980.

63. An extensive listing of international offices in Soviet government agencies may be found in *Directory of Soviet Officials, Volume I: National Organizations*, Central Intelligence Agency, CR 79-16593, November 1979. (Hereafter cited as *National Organizations Directory*.)

64. Triska and Finley, p. 36.

65. *National Organizations Directory*, pp. 130-132. Canada, New Zealand, and Australia come under the Second European Department, along with Ireland, Malta, and the United Kingdom.

66. *Directory of USSR Ministry of Foreign Affairs Officials*, Central Intelligence Agency, CR 80-13493, August 1980, pp. 28-29. (Hereafter cited as *MFA Directory*.)

67. Triska and Finley, p. 37; ànd Aleksandr Kaznacheev, *Inside a Soviet Embassy*, J. B. Lippincott Co., New York, 1962, pp. 184-185.

68. Ibid., p. 38; and *MFA Directory*, p. ix.

69. Kaznacheev, Chap. 1.

70. For details of the five major functions, see Louvan E. Nolting, *The Structure and Functions of the U.S.S.R. State Committee for Science and Technology*, U.S. Department of Commerce, Foreign Economic Report, No. 16, November 1979. (Hereafter cited as *S&T Committee Structure*.)

71. The close relationship with the intelligence services that such tasks entail are discussed in the subsection on intelligence services.

72. *S&T Committee Structure*, p. 17, and Lawrence H. Theriot, "U.S. Governmental and Private Industry Cooperation with the Soviet Union in the Fields of Science and Technology," in U.S. Congress, Joint Economic Committee, *Soviet Economy in a New Perspective*, October 14, 1976, p. 744. (Hereafter cited as *Soviet Economy in a New Perspective*.)

73. *S&T Committee Structure*, p. 17.

74. *Soviet Economy in a New Perspective*, p. 744.

75. Conversation with David Ross, Central Intelligence Agency.

76. Ibid.

77. This discussion of foreign area specialists in functional ministries owes much to the knowledge and experience of Scott Blacklin, who lived and worked in Moscow for a long period as the commercial representative of U.S. firms.

78. Triska and Finley, pp. 59-60.

79. For a complete listing of the Central Committee departments, see *National Organizations Directory*. This section covers only Moscow-based activities of Central Committee foreign area specialists. For a discussion of the important role such specialists play abroad, see below, pp. 110-111.

80. Darrell P. Hammer, *USSR: Politics of Oligarchy*, The Dryden Press, Hinsdale, Ill., 1974, p. 383.

81. Leonard Shapiro, "The International Department of the CPSU: Key to Soviet Policy," *International Journal* (Canadian Institute of International Affairs, Toronto), Vol. 32, No. 1, Winter 1976-1977, pp. 41ff.

82. Ben Fischer, "The Soviet Political System and Foreign Policy-Making in the Brezhnev Era," in Seweryn Bialer (ed.), *The Domestic Context of Soviet Foreign Policy*, Collection of papers prepared at the Research Institute on International Change, Columbia University, in collaboration with the Hudson Institute, under Department of State contract 1722-620179, May 1979, p. 326.

83. Shapiro, p. 44.

84. Ibid.

85. Fischer, pp. 329-330.

86. See Section 2, notes 21 and 68.

87. Fischer, p. 330.

88. Ibid., p. 331.

89. We are grateful to Lilita Dzirkals of The Rand Corporation for this information.

90. Dzirkals.

91. V. G. Kulikov (ed.), *Akademiya General'nogo shtaba* (General Staff Academy), Voyenizdat, Moscow, 1976, p. 13. The educational task of the General Staff Academy is described on p. 45.

92. Kulikov, p. 5.

93. We noted above that the Military Institute trains analysts and translators for military service. We assume, therefore, that many western military journals, books, and other materials are translated into Russian. However, we think it unlikely that an analyst at the General Staff Academy would be able to find in Russian translation everything he needed for a research project.

94. Harriet Fast Scott and William F. Scott, *The Armed Forces of the USSR*, Westview Press, Boulder, Colorado, 1979, p. 354.

95. Thomas W. Wolfe, *The SALT Experience*, Ballinger Publishing Co., Cambridge, Mass., 1979, pp. 62, 64.

96. Ibid., p. 64.

97. *Communist Aid Activities in Non-Communist Less Developed Countries, 1979 and 1954-79*, Central Intelligence Agency, ER 80-10318U, October 1980, p. 5. Additional discussion of Soviet military missions abroad can be found on pp. 141-142.

98. Ibid., p. 6.

99. See pp. 78-80.

100. S. G. Gorshkov, *Morskaya moshch' gosudarstva* (The Sea Power of the State), Voyenizdat, Moscow, 1979, p. 372. Gorshkov cites a Kenyan newspaper to the effect that Soviet sailors do not create chaos in port as do their American and British counterparts. Thus, we get the picture of sailors cowed into unsailor-like behavior by the solemnity of their civic duties. Whether or not this picture is accurate, we know that Soviet sailors are tightly controlled in port. For an idea of how

that control extends to currency matters, see B. Smyslov, "Strogo soblyudat' tamozhennyye pravila" (Strictly Observe Customs Laws), *Morskoy sbornik*, No. 9, 1980.

101. Political officers are outside the regular naval hierarchy in that they are subordinate to the Main Political Administration of the Soviet Army and Navy (MPA) as well as to the commander of their vessel. They are trained by the MPA.

102. *Communist Aid Activities in Non-Communist Less Developed Countries, 1979 and 1954-79*, p. 6.

103. Oleg Penkovskiy, *The Penkovskiy Papers*, Doubleday & Co., Garden City, N.Y., 1965, p. 66.

104. We are grateful to Harry Gelman of The Rand Corporation for his insights on this matter.

105. Harry Rositzke, *The KGB: The Eyes of Russia*, Doubleday & Co., Garden City, N.Y., 1981, p. 194.

106. Ibid., p. 187.

107. Ibid., p. 230. Dr. John Dziak of DIA also mentioned the language wage differentials in an interview.

108. John Barron, *KGB: The Secret Work of Soviet Secret Agents*, Reader's Digest Press, New York, 1974, p. 21.

109. Rositzke, p. 53.

110. Barron, pp. 78-79.

111. Ibid., p. 79.

112. Ibid., pp. 81-82. See Barron, pp. 70-90, for a more detailed description of the administrative breakdown of the KGB.

113. Rositzke, p. xii; see also Barron, pp. 76-77.

114. We appreciate Dr. John Dziak's evaluation of the analysis issue.

115. Penkovskiy, p. 172.

116. Ibid., p. 179.

117. Barron, pp. 76, 102.

118. Ibid., p. 102.

119. Penkovskiy, p. 174.

120. Rositzke, p. 184.

121. Conversation with John Dziak.

122. See Aleksandr Kaznacheev, op. cit., and Vladimir Sakharov, *High Treason*, G. P. Putnam's Sons, New York, 1980.

123. The possibility of bias in emigre authors' accounts has been considered in writing the section, and we hope that readers will consider it also.

124. Kaznacheev (Ch. 8, especially p. 96) gives an explicit account of this double subordination. Sakharov (pp. 196-199) affirms that the system still existed in the late 1960s and early 1970s.

125. The Ministry of Foreign Affairs and its representatives abroad are mentioned here only in passing, first, because the ministry's structure and function parallel those of other diplomatic services, except for its Tenth Department (discussed above, pp. 107-109) and, second, because Kaznacheev, Sakharov, and others have noted the unimportance of MFA diplomats relative to other Soviet representatives abroad. See Kaznacheev, pp. 199-202, and Sakharov, p. 196. For the structure of the MFA, see above, pp. 87-88 and Section III, note 66.

126. Kaznacheev, pp. 97-107. TASS is discussed above, pp. 99-101.

127. Sakharov, pp. 248-250. Both authors agree that all missions have a large intelligence function, which ministry employees as well as KGB or GRU officers perform.

128. Kaznacheev, p. 97.

129. Ibid.

130. Kaznacheev, pp. 98, 182.

131. Sakharov, p. 155.

132. Ibid. Sakharov gives many pungent examples of poor behavior by Soviet technical specialists. See, for example, pp. 231, 251.

133. *Communist Aid Activities in Non-Communist Less Developed Countries, 1979 and 1954-79*, pp. 3, 10. In 1979, they were employed as follows: heavy industry, 40 percent; teaching, 19 percent; power and irrigation, 17 percent; geology, 6 percent; agriculture, 5 percent; doctors, 5 percent; and other, 8 percent.

134. Ibid., pp. 8-9. According to Sakharov (p. 222), Soviet workers in Egypt in 1969 were paid less than half of what their work was billed for.

135. Kaznacheev, pp. 98-99; Sakharov, p. 179. Sakharov goes so far as to say that every aid project is "a KGB Trojan horse," p. 87.

136. Triska and Finley, p. 42. We should note, however, that the State Committee for Science and Technology seems to have the lead role in formulating policy involving technological assistance for the developing countries. See above, pp. 88-90.

137. See above, pp. 108-109.

138. *National Organizations Directory*, pp. 267-271.

139. Kaznacheev, p. 99.

140. Ibid., pp. 100-101.

141. Sakharov, p. 250.

142. A State Department official who recently returned from Moscow told us that a young Russian couple of his acquaintance had been fortunate in being assigned to Algeria, where husband and wife could both earn hard currency. He teaches technical subjects and she Russian language. Kaznacheev and Sakharov describe the use to which hard currency earnings are put. See Kaznacheev, Ch. 5, and Sakharov, p. 222.

143. Triska and Finley, p. 43. As mentioned earlier, the CIA estimates that 5 percent of Soviet economic technicians in less developed countries in 1979 were doctors. In addition, 30,970 academic students from these countries were being trained in the USSR at the end of 1979. See *Communist Aid Activities in Non-Communist Less Developed Countries, 1979 and 1954-79*, pp. 3, 22.

144. Sakharov, p. 250.

145. Ibid., pp. 248ff. See also *Die Welt*, November 1, 1975.

146. Shapiro, p. 43.

147. Sakharov, p. 155.

148. According to the CIA, this switch occurred after Israel's deep penetration of Egypt in 1970. The Soviets now sometimes offer expensive new equipment to Third World countries even before they export it to their East European allies. *Communist Aid Activities in Non-Communist Less Developed Countries, 1979 and 1954-79*, pp. 4-5.

149. Ibid., p. 6.

150. Triska and Finley, p. 52.

151. Stalin argued at the end of World War II that each Soviet republic should be represented separately. The Ukrainian and Belorussian delegations emerged as the compromise. Ibid., p. 5.

152. These activities seem mostly to involve keeping abreast of changes in U.S. fisheries policy. Before the Carter administration cut Soviet quotas for fish to zero after the invasion of Afghanistan, they also engaged in lobbying.

153. See, for example, "Soviet Defector, on BBC, Says Moscow Agents Have Penetrated the U.N.," *The New York Times*, September 25, 1979.

154. Promising sources of information include the reports of the U.S. Bureau of East-West Trade, the CIA, the Confederation of British Industry, the Ostausschuss der Deutschen Wirtschaft, the Centre Français du Commerce Extérieur, and the Office Belge pour Commerce Extérieur, as well as certain publications of the Japanese Ministry of International Trade and Industry and of a number of nonofficial Japanese associations concerned with East-West trade. Useful data may also be obtained from a systematic examination of *Ekonomicheskaya gazeta, Vneshnyaya torgovlya, Moscow Narodny Bank Press Bulletin, Soviet Business and Trade*, and *East-West Markets*. Among academic studies, the high quality analyses of the Institute of Soviet and East European Studies at Carleton University, Ottawa, deserve particular attention.

155. "Diagramma rosta torgovli SSSR" (Diagram of USSR Trade Growth), *Vneshnyaya torgovlya SSSR v 1979 g.*, Moscow, 1980, p. 6. According to Soviet statistics, about half of this turnover is accounted for by economic exchanges with the CMEA (Council of Mutual Economic Assistance) countries, the economies of which are being integrated with those of the USSR. (Brezhnev reported at the 26th CPSU Congress in February 1981 that the process of integration "is gathering momentum" and that about 120 multilateral and over 1000 bilateral agreements had been concluded. "Coordination of the CMEA countries' national-economic plans for 1981-1985 is nearing completion," *Pravda* and *Izvestiya*, February 24, 1981. An English translation may be found in *Current Digest of the Soviet Press* beginning with the issue of March 25, 1981.) Given the Soviet political-military domination of the CMEA countries or at least of those in Eastern Europe, it is not clear to what extent the Soviet bureaucratic apparatus sees fit to employ experts with specialized training regarding these countries. In the case of the East European nations, communications with the USSR appear to be predominantly in Russian.

156. *Vneshnyaya torgovlya SSSR v 1979 g.*, pp. 9-14, lists 96 countries, distributed geographically as follows: Europe (both CMEA and outside the Soviet orbit)--26; Asia--29; Africa--26; Americas--13; Australia and Oceania--2. *USSR Facts and Figures Annual*, drawing on earlier volumes of the above Soviet reference work, lists 106 countries figuring in Soviet foreign trade.

157. *Ekonomicheskaya gazeta*, February 9, 1981, translated in FBIS, *Daily Report--USSR*, February 25, 1981.

158. See *USSR Facts and Figures Annual*, pp. 25-27.

159. The division of responsibility in this area between the Ministry of Foreign Trade and the State Committee for Science and Technology is discussed above, pp. 110-111.

160. See above, pp. 106-107.

161. See Carl H. McMillan, *Direct Soviet and East European Investment in the Industrialized Western Economies*, Institute of Soviet and East European Studies (East-West Commercial Relations Series), Carleton University, Ottawa, Canada, February 1977.

162. It is our impression that, as in the Soviet diplomatic service, foreign area specialization is regularly reflected in trade assignments abroad, i.e., country or regional expertise is fully taken into account except on the highest policymaking levels of the economic bureaucracy.

163. On April 9, 1981, *Pravda* reported the inauguration of a Moscow-Freetown (Sierra Leone) passenger route, the 86th regular Aeroflot link between the Soviet capital and the capitals of foreign countries.

164. Ralph Ostrich, "Aeroflot," *Armed Forces Journal*, No. 9, May 1981, p. 40.

165. McMillan, p. 3.

166. Carl H. McMillan, "Soviet Investment in the Industrialized Western Economies and in the Developing Economies of the Third World," in U.S. Congress, Joint Economic Committee, *Soviet Economy in a Time of Change*, Vol. 2, October 10, 1979, pp. 628-629.

167. See Chris Blackburn, "Joint Venture Expects Expansion," Kodiak (Alaska) *Daily Mirror*, December 2, 1980, and E. Allison and Yu. Sergeyev, "Close Cooperation," *Nakhodkinskiy rabochiy*, February 1981. See also Linda Schild, "Local Firm Joins with Soviet Union in Fishing Venture," Bellingham (Washington) *Herald*, August 5, 1976.

168. McMillan, October 1979, p. 643.

169. Ibid., p. 626.

170. Maureen R. Smith, "Industrial Cooperation Agreements: Soviet Experience and Practice," in U.S. Congress, Joint Economic Committee, *Soviet Economy in a New Perspective*, October 14, 1976, p. 770.

171. Teacher exchanges are described in the section on education, pp. 66-69. Foreign area activities of the State Committee for Science and Technology are described on pp. 88-90. Aspects of various academic research exchanges have also been noted in preceding sections.

172. FBIS, *Daily Report--USSR*, April 14, 1981, p. K2; and May 1, 1981, p. H7.

173. IREX, *Annual Report, 1977-1978*, pp. 7, 17, and Felice D. Gaer, "Soviet-American Scholarly Exchange: Should Learning and Politics Mix?" *Vital Issues*, No. 10, June 1980, p. 7.

174. For an excellent, detailed description of both types of exchange, see *Soviet Economy in a New Perspective*, pp. 739-766.

175. Gaer, p. 11.

176. See *National Organizations Directory*, p. 101.

177. For a discussion of the relationship between these organizations and the International Department of the CPSU Central Committee, see pp. 117-118, 141.

178. For a list of the friendship societies and information on other propaganda and foreign liaison organizations, see *National Organizations Directory*, pp. 373-380.

179. Gaer, p. 7.

IV. CONCLUSIONS

This study has examined the training and career potential of Soviet citizens whose jobs bring them in contact with foreigners, foreign information, foreign technology, and other aspects of the world outside the USSR. The study has also reviewed the language and area training that every Soviet student receives beginning in primary school and continuing through secondary and higher education. We draw upon these discussions here to form conclusions about the training and utilization of Soviet foreign area specialists.

Our conclusions are grouped under the topics of general foreign area training, specialized foreign area training, full-time foreign area specialists, and double area specialists. We identify significant aspects of each topic, especially as they relate to differences in the U.S. and Soviet systems. We pose several important questions that emerged during the course of our research, questions that we feel deserve closer study. Finally, we suggest a few areas where the Soviet experience may be applicable to the United States.

GENERAL FOREIGN LANGUAGE AND AREA TRAINING IN THE USSR

Everyone in the USSR is officially exposed to some form of foreign language and area training during his education. This training program offers advantages to the USSR that the elective system prevailing in the United States either fails to provide or provides less well.

Soviet foreign language requirements apply country-wide; therefore, even if they are not always met, the USSR has a gigantic pool of schoolchildren studying foreign languages, culture, history, and geography from which to choose talent for specialized training in the international field.

Mass foreign area training gives the USSR a population with a large latent foreign language capability. Theoretically, this capability could be revived in times of national need--although in reality it may be difficult to awaken long-dormant language skills. The infrastructure for such a revival nevertheless already exists in the large corps of

foreign language teachers skilled in the major languages taught in the
USSR, especially English, German, and French.

Furthermore, because they are assured of continued work in their
chosen field, Soviet language teachers can afford to be devoted to it.
The existence of a stable language·teacher population alone means that
significant language capability can be quickly made available, say, in
wartime, when a large number of military translators would be needed.

Universal exposure in the classroom to foreign languages and cultures, although bounded by the requirements of Marxism-Leninism, to some
extent counteracts the closed nature of Soviet society. The effect may
be magnified if students seek outside contacts through various means--
practicing English on tourists, listening to foreign radio broadcasts,
reading foreign magazines, etc.

Soviet leaders probably feel ambivalent about this "society-
opening" consequence of foreign area training. However, they doubtless
hesitate to alter the language and area curricula because the Soviet
state derives considerable advantages from them.

SPECIALIZED FOREIGN LANGUAGE AND AREA TRAINING IN THE USSR

The Soviet educational system also provides specialized foreign
language and area training, from primary grades through graduate school.
Primary and secondary schoolchildren can attend special language schools
throughout the country, and secondary school graduates can find many
foreign area programs at institutes and universities.

Probably the most important aspect of specialized foreign area
training in the USSR is its tremendous variety. This variety is especially evident in programs designed to train full-time internationalists.
Students interested in the developing countries, for example, can study
exotic Asian, African, and Middle Eastern languages, along with the more
traditionally studied languages of Europe and the Far East.

Double area specialists also receive significant language training,
but it appears to be less varied than of the full-time area specialists.
Many scientists, for example, concentrate on learning languages in which
a large volume of scientific literature is printed abroad, namely,
English, German, and French. We were unable to determine whether double

area specialists working abroad, say, geologists prospecting for oil in the Middle East, learn the local languages. The evidence of their college curricula points to European languages, especially English.

Whether or not the double area specialists acquire the esoteric qualifications of the full-time area specialists, we find it interesting that foreign language studies are an important part of their education. No matter what field he chooses, an aspiring Soviet scientist studies foreign languages systematically, usually for three years.

This appreciation for the usefulness of foreign languages in scientific and technical fields contrasts sharply with the prevailing viewpoint in the United States. Of course, English is an international language of science--but it is not the only one.

Soviet foreign area specialist training also has serious shortcomings. Students cannot count on routine travel outside the USSR. Junior-year-abroad programs or summer backpacking trips through Europe are unheard of in the Soviet system. In addition, routine student contacts with foreigners inside the USSR are probably not encouraged. Thus, Soviet students of foreign affairs are generally denied the ease of language comprehension and cultural understanding that comes with foreign travel and contacts.

To remedy this situation, Soviet educators have devised a system of practical training abroad. This training, which usually occurs late in the student's education, takes on the nature of a preemployment internship. A variety of institutions sponsor practical training programs, including the Institute of the Countries of Asia and Africa at Moscow State University, the Moscow State Institute of International Relations, and the Institute of the United States and Canada.

The institutions offering practical training are the prestigious schools that turn out foreign area specialists. For this reason, we feel that the elite among aspiring Soviet internationalists probably are adequately compensated for the lack of routine travel and contacts, but that other students of foreign affairs may remain seriously disadvantaged by the closed nature of the Soviet system.

FOREIGN AREA SPECIALIZATION: USSR vs. UNITED STATES

Full-time foreign area specialists in the USSR, like those in the
United States, form a well-trained, diverse professional cadre, ready
to respond to policymakers and others who need information on a wide
range of countries. However, the significant political, economic, and
social differences between the two countries lead to differences in the
nature of the foreign affairs field in each.

First, the foreign area specialty is one of the few Soviet professions that allow contacts with foreigners and travel abroad. Many foreign area jobs in fact probably preclude such activities. For example,
intelligence analysts based in the USSR may not be allowed to leave the
country. A young Soviet planning his career, however, probably finds
the possibility of travel and foreign friends attractive.

In other words, the profession offers powerful perquisites to members of Soviet society who may see no other opportunities for foreign
experience. Because of these perquisites, the caliber of those attracted
to the field is likely to be high.

A second factor that probably engenders enthusiasm for the field
involves secure demand for foreign area specialists. Each young Soviet
admitted to foreign area training knows that a foreign area job, perhaps
an exciting one, awaits him on graduation. The relatively risk-free
nature of the career choice, coupled with the advantages mentioned above,
may make foreign area specialists among the most motivated professionals
in the USSR.

The foreign affairs field is less secure in the United States than
in the USSR, and U.S. specialists may therefore consider it a less desirable career than do their Soviet counterparts. A recent Rand study
showed a considerable lag in the United States between the number of
people training for work in foreign affairs and those able to find jobs
in the field.[1] Furthermore, although a foreign area career in the U.S.
may make travel and contacts more frequent than is normally the case,
such activities are not limited to those in the international field.
Thus, it seems likely that the motivation and enthusiasm of U.S. foreign
area specialists arise from sources other than those inspiring their
Soviet counterparts.

Does this difference affect the performance of foreign area specialists in the two countries? Are U.S. specialists less motivated because they are unsure of finding jobs? Are Soviet specialists any more
motivated for the opposite reason? Does the caliber of people entering
the field differ in each country according to the relative attractions
it offers? These are important questions, but they are outside the
scope of this study.

The secure demand factor has another important effect on the profession in the USSR. Basically, secure demand for specialists in a
large number of exotic areas ensures a trend toward diversity in the
Soviet international field. The system recognizes that numerous Africa,
Latin America, China, and Middle East specialists--as well as Americanists and Europeanists--are needed on a constant basis. This diversity does not exist in the same measure in the United States, where the
need for specialists in exotic languages and cultures is often felt
only during crises.[2]

DOUBLE AREA SPECIALIZATION: USSR vs. UNITED STATES

The double area specialist represents a phenomenon much more common
in the USSR than in the United States. Soviet scientists, engineers,
managers, and others anticipate rewards, including career advancement
and perquisites, for language and area skills. Therefore, they consider
acquiring such skills a worthwhile expenditure of time and effort.

A knowledge of foreign languages and foreign countries matters
less in the United States--and for good reason. English is the most
common language in international scientific and commercial discourse,
and it is also widely used in diplomacy and nonscientific areas of academia. Thus, Americans rarely feel the same need to learn foreign languages that Europeans, including Russians, feel.

However, Americans may want to consider some advantages that the
Soviets derive from having scientists, engineers, and managers who are
double area specialists. Perhaps most important, Soviets with a wide
range of specialties have potential access to published materials covering many subjects in many languages. These specialists can use information that comes their way directly, without the handicap of poor or

tardy translations. This capability to utilize foreign materials counterbalances, to a certain extent, the closed nature of Soviet society
for scientists, engineers, and other professionals.

On a much smaller scale, some double area specialists gain direct
access to foreign professionals, research facilities, and manufacturing
plants through cooperation and exchange agreements. With their language
and area skills, these specialists can profit directly from their experiences abroad, once again bypassing the handicap imposed by dependence on
translation. For example, a Soviet researcher interested in applying
computer methods to economic analysis can potentially work directly with
western colleagues in a university economics department, unencumbered by
the need for an interpreter.

The crucial issue here, we feel, involves the "hands-on" opportunities potentially available to a language-skilled specialist. His access
to foreign colleagues can be much greater than that of a specialist with
no languages, who must depend on an interpreter and thus can easily end
up a passive observer. The ability among double area specialists to
utilize foreign travel more efficiently, like the ability to use foreign
information, counterbalances somewhat the effect of the closed Soviet
society.

UNANSWERED QUESTIONS

During the course of our research, many questions emerged that we
could not answer within the scope of this study. Most of these questions
were raised--some more than once--where they occurred in the body of the
report. We review them here.

A question that recurred several times concerns the overall issue
of effectiveness. The Soviet leadership has evidently become increasingly satisfied with the cadre of foreign area specialists that advises it.
High-level specialists have gained at least partial entree to the Soviet
policymaking establishment, and the institutes with which they are affiliated are no longer subjected to party-imposed reorganizations. Under
these new conditions, the international field has been able to grow and
flourish in the Soviet environment.

We wonder, however, if that growth implies increased effectiveness in the same measure. Soviet internationalists continue to misperceive and misunderstand the West, and their analyses often seem less dictated by reality than by ideological considerations. Unfortunately, we cannot judge the extent to which such misperceptions and skewed analyses affect Kremlin decisionmaking. What appears in the open press and in conversations with Soviets may differ in accuracy and sophistication from what appears on the desks of Soviet leaders.

Perhaps more important, what appears to a westerner to be a misperception may seem to be a fact to a Soviet weaned on Marxism-Leninism. This accuracy and perception aspect of the effectiveness question will seem familiar to any student of international affairs. Nevertheless, it is a thorny problem in the Soviet case, and one that we were unable adequately to address.

A second aspect of the effectiveness question concerns the roles that the USSR allows its non-Russian republics to play in the training and utilization of specialists. Like other fields, the Soviet international field seems to be centered in Moscow. However, we found well-established centers for Turkic and Oriental studies in Central Asia and the Far East. Does that fact imply that the Soviets are making particularly effective use of native language and area capabilities in those regions?

Stories abound concerning the part that Central Asians played in the Soviet invasion of Afghanistan. Soviet military commanders may not have found the Uzbeks to be good soldiers, but they may have found them to be good translators. Furthermore, since the invasion, scores of Afghan students have been sent to study in the USSR, many in the Central Asian republics. Perhaps the Soviet leadership has decided that study in the USSR is the best way to orient them to Soviet-style socialism. Central Asia and Afghanistan are a ready example, but they by no means preclude the participation of other non-Russian nationalities in Soviet international activities that would benefit from native language and area skills.

The performance of Soviet personnel abroad is a third aspect of effectiveness that we must question. We know that the Soviets send

foreign area specialists, such as language teachers, abroad, and we know
that they send double area specialists, such as economic aid personnel,
abroad. The former are highly trained in language and area studies, and
the latter are probably somewhat trained in language and area studies.
For neither, however, do we have an adequate measure of effectiveness.

In the case of military aid personnel, we have even less information.
We know that large numbers of them are serving in the Third World, but we
have no idea if they receive any special training to do so. Furthermore,
we do not know how well they interact with their foreign clients, i.e.,
whether they are forging deep friendships or merely maintaining marriages
of convenience.

Full answers to the effectiveness question are not easy to come by.
However, we feel that it would be possible to develop useful partial
answers through talking with those who have come in contact with Soviets
both at home and abroad, but especially in developing countries.[3] American diplomatic and aid personnel, businessmen and bankers, and technicians employed by commercial firms are all potential sources of information. Likewise, U.S. military attaches serving in countries where the
Soviets are active should have some impression of their effectiveness at
cultural interaction. We believe that it would be possible to produce
some measure of the effectiveness of Soviet personnel working abroad.

Our second question concerns the distribution of double area specialists among the sectors of the Soviet economy. We suspect that sectors employing large numbers of double area specialists—management
theory, computers, and chemicals—are the focus of particular Soviet
efforts to improve economic performance. Double area specialists would
be the tools to effect that improvement. Specialists on western management techniques, for example, may be needed to help ease a turnkey
plant into production after its U.S. builders have departed. Such specialists would be expediting a technology transfer. Other specialists—
in the chemical field, for example—may be more involved in keeping
abreast of western developments to be replicated in the USSR. Theirs
would be an information function.

Whether for technology transfer, data assimilation, or other purposes, double area specialists hold many jobs in the Soviet economy.

We would like to have a better idea of what sectors employ them, and why. Once again, a partial source of this information would be people who have worked alongside Soviets, such as businessmen and embassy commercial officers.

The literature of the various fields would also give some indication of where double area specialists are employed. Soviet military journals reveal abundant coverage of western military literature. Are other fields covered to such an extent? An answer to that question might provide evidence of Soviet interest in improving performance in those fields.

Our final question returns to the matter of effectiveness and concerns an important limitation in the Soviet training and utilization of foreign area specialists. In this study, we have noted the Soviets' attempts to counteract certain restrictions of their closed society. In the training sphere, practical experience abroad is the instrument. In the utilization sphere, the specialists themselves become the instruments--or perhaps mirrors--through which Soviet society sees the world. Both endeavors, we feel, provide only limited benefits.

During training, relatively few aspiring foreign specialists are sent abroad for practical experience. Once graduated, these same elite few are again apparently the only members of the field likely to travel outside the USSR. Most Soviet foreign area professionals, in other words, never visit the countries in which they specialize. Because of this limitation, we wonder how effectively they reflect the outside world.

Of course, we can never completely resolve this issue, especially since we are looking at the Soviet international field through western eyes. Soviet policymakers evidently are satisfied with their foreign area specialists: they continue to train and utilize them in large numbers. That continued utilization, of course, is one way to gauge the effectiveness of foreign area specialists.

APPLICABILITY OF THE SOVIET EXPERIENCE TO THE UNITED STATES

What benefit can the international field in the United States derive from the Soviet experience of training and utilizing foreign area specialists? Clearly, some Soviet uses of the profession would be unnecessary or inappropriate in the U.S. context. It would probably be a waste, for example, to replicate the legions of Soviet double area specialists who follow foreign scientific developments. Because the communications network among scientists in the West is fairly well-developed, in most cases U.S. scientists need not be double area specialists.

A selective adoption of Soviet practices, however, might help U.S. scientists, policymakers, and others. For example, we think that the double area specialist phenomenon gives the Soviet government a certain flexibility that would be useful for the U.S. government to have as well. Soviet policymakers can turn for advice directly to Soviet double area specialists in a number of fields, rather than depending on internationalists who may not have specialized knowledge. U.S.-trained double area specialists could provide a similar service, especially in scientific and technical fields where internationalists tend to lack expertise.

In the United States, the climate for double area specialists could be improved simply by encouraging--or requiring--more foreign language studies in noninternational academic programs. We are not suggesting, of course, that language requirements would increase interest in foreign science and technology among U.S. science students. More language-skilled graduates, however, would provide policymakers with the raw material for developing double area expertise in the scientific population, should the need for them arise. In other words, we think that developing potential capability in this sphere may be as important as developing actual capability.

Aspects of Soviet foreign area training are also useful for U.S. policymakers to consider. For example, we described how certain foreign area institutes sponsor internships in Soviet embassies and missions abroad. The apparent scale of these internship programs would be difficult to duplicate in the U.S. case, because the structure of the foreign service and the expense of housing in foreign capitals dictate against it. Likewise, embassy-connected internships would not be necessary in many places where students can easily travel--Western Europe, Latin America, Japan. The internships would be most useful in countries that limit student travel--the USSR, China, and some countries of Africa.

A student serving as an intern in Moscow probably could not do the type of academic research that exchange scholars do, because he would not have access to libraries and archives. However, he would be gaining practical experience by living and working in the city and by performing free services for the Department of State or other sponsoring agency.

An informal internship arrangement has existed in Moscow for years. Many foreign diplomatic families there hire young women from their home country to work as nannies for one or two years. These young women use their free time to perfect their Russian, explore Moscow, and learn about Soviet life. Often, they later enter the Soviet field professionally.

This type of "internship," of course, is predicated on the existence of housing--many diplomatic families have servant quarters--and the willingness of the participants to work hard for little money. Expanding and adapting such a program on an official or semiofficial basis would be complicated, but we think not impossible.

Another example of Soviet practice in foreign area training that may be useful in the United States involves Patrice Lumumba University. Lumumba students from developing nations are provided with Soviet roommates for at least their first year. Both groups learn from the experience--the foreigners about Russian language and Soviet culture, the Soviets about individual countries in the Third World.

We think that a similar approach may work well at U.S. colleges that have programs in agricultural and economic aid and development. An American studying the agricultural problems of Africa, for example, may profit from the knowledge of an African exchange student. If the American has never traveled, an African roommate would give him his first exposure to the culture, language, and government system of at least one region of Africa. Such exposure would begin the process of producing a specialist on African agriculture.

Other examples in this study of Soviet training and utilization methods could be successfully adapted to the U.S. international field. Obviously, the training and utilization of foreign area specialists is a diverse, well-developed system in the USSR. It may not always work precisely, but it produces an array of specialists on a regular basis, and then it uses them. This lesson, we feel, is the basic one of our research and the most important.

Section IV Notes

1. Sue E. Berryman, Paul F. Langer, John Pincus, Richard H. Solomon, *Foreign Language and International Studies Specialists: The Marketplace and National Policy*, The Rand Corporation, R-2501-NEH, September 1979, p. vii.

2. Ibid.

3. Using such a technique, Gregory Guroff and Steven Grant of the United States Information Agency have already gained some important insights into the effectiveness of specialists employed in Moscow. The results of their surrogate interview projects are contained in Gregory Guroff, *Soviet Perceptions of the U.S.: Results of a Surrogate Interview Project*, United States Information Agency (USIA), Office of Research, M-16-80, June 27, 1980; Guroff, *Soviet Elite Sources of Information on the U.S.: Availability and Credibility*, USIA, Office of Research, M-33-80, November 26, 1980; Gregory Guroff and Steven Grant, *Soviet Elites: World View and Perceptions of the U.S.*, USIA, Office of Research, R-18-81, September 29, 1981.